DUMFRIES
AND
GALLOWAY

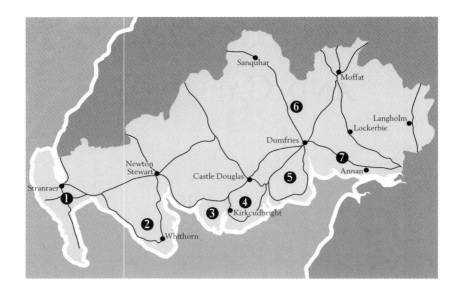

EXCURSIONS

EXPLORING SCOTLAND'S HERITAGE

RCAHMS

DUMFRIES
AND GALLOWAY

Geoffrey Stell

Series Editor: Anna Ritchie

EDINBURGH: THE STATIONERY OFFICE

Cover photography: Front, Caerlaverock Castle
Back, Whithorn (Crown copyright Historic Scotland)

End papers by Elisa Trimby

British Library Cataloguing in Publication Data

A catalogue record for this book is available from the British Library

Royal Commission on the Ancient and Historical Monuments of Scotland
John Sinclair House, 16 Bernard Terrace, Edinburgh EH8 9NX
0131-662 1456

The Royal Commission, which was established in 1908, is responsible for compiling a national record of archaeological sites and historic buildings of all types and periods. The Royal Commission makes this record available both through its publications (details of which can be obtained from the above address) and through the maintenance of a central archive of information, known as the National Monuments Record of Scotland. This contains the national collection of pictorial and documentary material relating to Scotland's ancient monuments and historic buildings and is open Monday to Friday for public reference at the above address.

The Stationery Office

Published by The Stationery Office and available from:
The Stationery Office Bookshops
71 Lothian Road Edinburgh EH3 9AZ
(counter service only)
South Gyle Crescent Edinburgh EH12 9EB
(mail, fax and telephone orders only)
0131-479 3141 Fax 0131-479 3142
49 High Holborn, London WC1V 6HB
(counter service and fax orders only)
Fax 0171-831 1326
68-69 Bull Street Birmingham B4 6AD
0121-236 9696 Fax 0121-236 9699
33 Wine Street Bristol BS1 2BQ
0117-926 4306 Fax 0117-929 4515
9-21 Princess Street Manchester M60 8AS
0161-834 7201 Fax 0161-833 0634
16 Arthur Street Belfast BT1 4GD
01232 238451 Fax 01232 235401
The Stationery Office Oriel Bookshop
The Friary Cardiff CF1 4AA
01222 395548 Fax 01222 384347

The Stationery Office publications are also available from:
The Publications Centre
(mail, telephone and fax orders only)
PO Box 276 London SW8 5DT
General enquiries 0171-873 0011
Telephone orders 0171-873 9090
Fax orders 0171-873 8200
Accredited Agents
(see Yellow Pages)
and through good booksellers

ALSO PUBLISHED

The Highlands

Argyll and The Western Isles

Aberdeen and North-East Scotland

Glasgow, Clydeside and Stirling

Fife, Perthshire and Angus

Orkney

OTHER TITLES IN PREPARATION

Shetland

Edinburgh, Lothians and The Borders

ISBN 0 11 495294 9

CONTENTS

**Port Logan
harbour**

FOREWORD

Scotland has a heritage of human endeavour stretching back some ten thousand years, and a wide range of man-made monuments survives as proof of that endeavour. The rugged character of much of the Scottish landscape has helped to preserve many antiquities which elsewhere have vanished beneath modern development or intensive deep ploughing, though with some 10,200 km of coastline there has also been an immeasurable loss of archaeological sites as a result of marine erosion. Above all, perhaps, the preservation of such a wide range of monuments should be credited to Scotland's abundant reserves of good building stone, allowing not only the creation of extraordinarily enduring prehistoric houses and tombs but also the development of such remarkable Scottish specialities as the medieval tower-house and the iron-age broch. This volume is one of a series of nine handbooks which have been designed to provide up-to-date and authoritative introductions to the rich archaeological heritage of the various regions of Scotland, highlighting the most interesting and best preserved of the surviving monuments and setting them in their original social context. The time-scale is the widest possible, from relics of World War II or the legacy of 19th-century industrial booms back through history and prehistory to the earliest pioneer days of human settlement, but the emphasis varies from region to region, matching the particular directions in which each has developed. Some monuments are still functioning (lighthouses for instance), others are still occupied as homes, and many have been taken into the care of the State or the National Trust for Scotland, but each has been chosen as specially deserving a visit.

Thanks to the recent growth of popular interest in these topics, there is an increasing demand for knowledge to be presented in a readily digestible form and at a moderate price. In sponsoring this series, therefore, the Royal Commission on the Ancient and Historical Monuments of Scotland broadens the range of its publications with the aim of making authentic information about the man-made heritage available to as wide an audience as possible. This is the second edition of the series, in which more monuments, museums and visitor centres have been added in order to reflect the way in which the management and presentation of Scotland's past have expanded over the last decade. The excursions section proved very popular and has been both expanded and illustrated in colour.

The author, Geoffrey Stell, has been a regular visitor to Dumfries and Galloway since 1960. He has made records of historic buildings in the region during his twenty-seven years with the Royal Commission on the Ancient and Historical Monuments of Scotland where he is Head of Architecture. He has made a special study of the Balliol family, one-time lords of Galloway, and has contributed to the proceedings of the Dumfriesshire and Galloway Natural History and Antiquarian Society.

Monuments have been grouped according to their character and date and, although only the finest, most interesting or best preserved have been described in detail, attention has also been drawn to other sites worth visiting in the vicinity. Each section has its own explanatory introduction, beginning with the most recent monuments and gradually retreating in time back to the earliest traces of prehistoric man.

Each major monument is numbered so that it may easily be located on the end-map, but it is recommended that the visitor should also use the relevant 1:50,000 maps published by the Ordnance Survey as its Landranger Series, particularly for the more remote sites. Sheet nos 71, 76, 77, 78, 79, 82, 83, 84 and 85 cover Dumfries and Galloway. The National Grid Reference for each site is provided (eg NW 975598) as well as local directions at the head of each entry.

An asterisk indicates that the site is subject to restricted hours of opening; unless attributed to Historic Scotland or the National Trust for Scotland (NTS), the visitor should assume the monument to be in private ownership **and should seek permission locally to view it.** It is of course vital that visitors to any monument should observe the country code and take special care to fasten gates. Where a church is locked, it is often possible to obtain the key from the local manse, post office or general store.

We have made an attempt to estimate how accessible each monument may be for disabled visitors, indicated at the head of each entry by a wheelchair logo and a number: 1=easy access for all visitors, including those in wheelchairs; 2=reasonable access for pedestrians but restricted access for wheelchairs; 3=restricted access for all disabled but a good view from the road or parking area; 4=access for the able-bodied only.

Many of the sites mentioned in this handbook are held in trust for the nation by the Secretary of State for Scotland and cared for on his behalf by Historic Scotland. Further information about these monuments, including details of guidebooks to individual properties, can be obtained from Historic Scotland, Longmore House, Salisbury Place, Edinburgh EH9 1SH. Information about properties in the care of the National Trust for Scotland can be obtained from the National Trust for Scotland, 5 Charlotte Square, Edinburgh EH2 4DU. The abbreviation NMS refers to the National Museums of Scotland, Chambers Street, Edinburgh, whose collections include important material from Dumfries and Galloway.

ANNA RITCHIE
Series Editor

ACKNOWLEDGEMENTS

My greatest debt in the preparation of this guide has been to my wife, Evelyn, and daughter, Katy, who have taught me to look at monuments through visitors' eyes, and who have guided the manuscript through a domestic word-processor. A special debt of gratitude is owed to my former colleague, Mr Geoffrey Hay, who commented on much of the work in progress and contributed a few of his peerless drawings. I also thank Mr John Dunbar for his kindness in reading the text of the first edition. The enthusiasm and hard work of my photographer colleagues, Mr John Keggie, Mr Jim Mackie and the dark-room staff, is gratefully acknowledged. I am also indebted to the series editor, Dr Anna Ritchie, for her guidance and forbearance. Mr Donald Urquhart, former Depute Director of Planning, Dumfries and Galloway Regional Council, has been an especially helpful source of local information.

For specific items of information, advice, and comment I should like to thank warmly the following: Miss Marilyn Brown; Mr Neil Cameron; the late Mr Richard Clarke; Mr Peter Corser; Miss Kitty Cruft; Mr Graham Douglas; Mr Ian Fisher; Mr Ian Fleming; Mr Ian Gow; Mr Simon Green; Mr Stratford Halliday; Mr Miles Horsey; Dr Aonghus McKechnie; Mr Gordon Maxwell; Mr Alastair Maxwell-Irving; Mr Robert Mowat; Dr Miles Oglethorpe; Dr Richard Oram; Dr Graham Ritchie; Mr Ian Scott; and the late Dr Ian Smith. I have also benefited considerably from an acquaintance with Mr Alfred Truckell, formerly Curator of Dumfries Burgh Museum and truly a living Gallovidian encyclopaedia!

Most of the photographs have been provided by the Royal Commission on the Ancient and Historical Monuments of Scotland (Photographic Department, and the archive of the National Monuments Record of Scotland), and these are Crown Copyright. For permission to reproduce photographs and drawings, author and publisher are gratefully indebted to the following institutions and individuals: Aerofilms (p. 140); Cambridge University Committee for Aerial Photography (pp. 128, 130, 134 top); Dumfries Museum (p.66); Dumfriesshire and Galloway Natural History and Antiquarian Society (pp. 86, 137, 159); Historic Scotland (pp. 12, 17, 20, 23 bottom, 37 bottom, 38, 40 bottom, 55, 76, 102, 110, 114 right, 116 bottom, 122 left and bottom right, 123, 150 bottom, 153 top, 154 top right and bottom, 155, 156 bottom, 158 top, 160, 161, 163, 164, 167, 169, 171, 172; Crown Copyright); Hopetoun House Trustees (p. 89); National Library of Scotland (p. 71, 116); Wanlockhead Museum Trust (p. 64); The Duke of Buccleuch (p. 50); R Clarke (p. 58); TE Gray (p. 142); GD Hay (pp. 53, 57, 65, 85, 118, 119 bottom); AMT Maxwell-Irving (pp. 111 middle, 112); Mrs Murray-Usher (p. 26 top); Mrs CM Piggott (p. 129); The Marquess of Salisbury (p. 108); M Sharp (pp. 47, 165); IM Smith (p. 41); and CW Stewart (p. 95). The photographs on pp. 35, 37 top, 43, 70, 137 and 176 were taken by the author.

**Sanquhar
Town House**

INTRODUCTION

Cairnsmore House by Mrs Henry Stuart, 1865

The landscape of Dumfries and Galloway possesses virtually all the scenic qualities that visitors expect to find in Scotland: a rugged mountainous heartland, hills and moorlands typical of the Border country, forests, lochs, glens, salmon rivers, and a long and fertile coastline which is washed by the Solway Firth and North Channel. In the west it also has a gentle undulating pastoral character strongly reminiscent of Ireland, and in the east the rich, deep farmlands of lower Annandale and Eskdale share the Solway Plain with northern Cumbria. Yet, whilst merging imperceptibly with its neighbours, the land at the heart of this region is subtly different from the rest of southern Scotland. What man has made of this landscape—and its changes—over the past seven millennia, and how that landscape has conditioned his efforts are major themes running through this guide. It is intended to show how the archaeology and historic architecture of the region share the cultural traditions of neighbouring provinces and of Scotland as a whole, and in what respects they are special and distinctive.

The chronology of human settlement broadly follows the general pattern encountered elsewhere in Scotland. The earliest evidence relates to itinerant communities of the remote mesolithic period, here traced back to camp-sites dating from about 4800 BC. They were succeeded by neolithic peoples (c 4000-2500 BC) whose achievements in this area are as yet measurable mainly by their ritual and burial practices rather than by their houses and farms. A similar limitation applies to the structures of the first metal-working peoples, those of the bronze age (broadly, 2500 to 700 BC), although their distinctive pottery and metal products give a progressively clearer picture of contemporary life-styles. The use of iron, from about the 7th century BC, ushered in an era of sophisticated fortification, accompanied by varieties of undefended settlements.

Monument in a Galloway landscape: Cairnholy II chambered cairn

In AD 79 Agricola, the governor of Roman Britain, extended the area of Roman control into southern Scotland. During the next two decades and intermittently thereafter in the 2nd and 3rd centuries his successors established a military occupation based upon a network of roads and forts. North of Hadrian's Wall, which was completed in the 120s, the main western trunk routes through Annandale and Nithsdale and their associated stations played a crucial role in this system until their abandonment towards the end of the 2nd century.

Post-Roman political history is marked by a succession of rulers who extended their control over the region: in the 6th and 7th centuries it formed part of the Celtic kingdom of Rheged; from the 8th to the 10th century most of the region was a colony of Anglian Northumbria; and in the 10th and 11th centuries it was prey to the activities of the Vikings and Gaelic-speaking Irish incomers (the *Gall-Ghaidhil*) who gave their name—and a reputation for toughness—to Galloway. Archaeologically, these centuries are dominated by the evidence of early Christianity which made its first recorded appearance in Scotland in late 4th- or early 5th-century Galloway. The Anglian and the Anglo-Norse periods are well represented, in some cases (no. 76) outstandingly, with Christian memorials.

With its own ruling dynasty of Gaelic-Norse descent, Galloway did not become a fully integrated part of the medieval Scottish kingdom until the 13th century, having been the target of royal military expeditions in the preceding century. Some eastern parts of the region, however, were among the first to be feudalised in 12th-century Scotland, lands being granted by the king to incomers such as the Bruces (at Annan in 1124) in return for what was originally defined as military service. This part of the region itself later experienced the effects of more than enough military service: the lands bordering the inner Solway were, until the Union of the Scottish and English Crowns in 1603, on the major invasion routes into western Scotland followed by English armies, a fact to which the fortifications and records of devastation bear equal witness. However, what is also especially evident from the monuments is the strong force of continuity and tradition which has underlain even the most dramatic upheavals in the region's history and ensured the long survival or adaptation of building styles and old beliefs.

It is worth bearing in mind the historical and functional links which have joined together different classes of monument in earlier times. To the modern mind, it is easy to grasp the interdependence between transport and trade, agriculture and industry, and the profits and losses on which towns and country houses have thrived or decayed. However, it is equally easy to overlook the ramifications of corporate or family power and wealth in the Middle Ages; a Douglas family connection joined Threave Castle (no. 38) and Lincluden Collegiate Church (no. 66), for example, and the region's three major monasteries were all Cistercian, one of the biggest and most highly organised of the medieval religious orders.

Physically, the region is intersected by a series of valleys in which the rivers drain southwards into the Solway: principally (from east to west) the Rivers Esk, Annan, Nith, Urr, Dee, Fleet, Cree, and their tributaries. Western

Galloway includes the broad headland known as the Machars (*Machair*, plain), and terminates in the hammer-headed promontory of the Rhins (*Rinn*, point, headland) whose southernmost tip, the Mull of Galloway, is the Land's End of Scotland.

The area covered by Dumfries and Galloway comprises the former counties of Dumfriesshire, Stewartry of Kirkcudbright, and Wigtownshire. Galloway consists of the 'Shire' (Wigtownshire) and the Stewartry bounded on the east by the River Nith and its catchment area around the head waters of the Urr; in fact, the eastern boundary of the medieval diocese of Galloway came to be fixed on the valley of the Urr itself. The Stewartry is a nominal historical title harking back to the time when, after the forfeiture of the Douglases in 1455, this lordship or regality was administered for the Crown by a steward, whose position was analogous to that of a sheriff.

The built heritage described in this volume is, of course, only part of a great human bequest which can be appreciated in documents and books as well as in fields and streets. This guide cannot take adequate account of a whole range of achievements—academic, artistic, business, linguistic, literary, military, political, social—nor even give a proper measure of the output and international stature of the region's most famous engineering son, Thomas Telford (d. 1834; no. 5). Nor, conversely, can the obelisk on Queen's Hill north of Ringford (NX 687607), easily seen from the A 75, give any measure of the physical impact of the person it commemorates, James Beaumont Neilson (d. 1865), a Glasgow man who spent his retirement here after his invention of the hot blast process in the manufacture of iron had begun to transform the industrial face of central Scotland.

Houses and places do, however, give insights into the work of literary creation: the area around Dumfries (nos 11, 21, 61) has strong associations with the last years of Robert Burns (d. 1796); Thomas Carlyle (d. 1881) was born and buried at Ecclefechan (no. 17); and Sir Walter Scott (d. 1832) fully exploited the romantic and antiquarian possibilities of the region through his local informant, Joseph Train (d. 1852) who lived in Castle Douglas. Galloway has been an inspiration to a whole succession of modern writers, including John Buchan (*Thirty-Nine Steps*) and Dorothy L Sayers (*Five Red Herrings*). It has also been home to, among others, Samuel Rutherford Crockett (d. 1914, buried in Balmaghie churchyard, NX 723663, and commemorated by a monument in Laurieston), and to the author and naturalist, Gavin Maxwell (d. 1969), whose autobiographical account, *The House of Elrig*, evokes the atmosphere and surroundings of his Galloway boyhood home. In the east of the region, Langholm lays proud claim to being the birthplace of the doyen of modern Scottish poets, Hugh MacDiarmid (d. 1978), born Christopher Murray Grieve in the block known as Library Buildings in the centre of the town.

The region has long accustomed itself to visitors, although only in the last few centuries have the incomers' intentions been consistently peaceable. A handful of Englishmen left short accounts of their travels in this area in the 17th century; the numbers and lengths of the travel-diaries increased in the 18th century, those by Daniel Defoe (*c* 1700), Sir John Clerk (1721, 1735),

Richard Pococke, Bishop of Ossory, later Meath (1750, 1760), Thomas Pennant (1772), and Robert Heron, a native (1792), being especially informative on antiquities, buildings and building customs. Then, as now, the roads from the south through Annandale and Nithsdale were busy with travellers heading for central Scotland and the Highlands, but Galloway itself lay comparatively unexplored by tourist traffic until the completion of the railway network in the 1860s and 1870s.

In the 18th and 19th centuries, the medicinal properties of sulphureous and chalybeate springs were always a powerful tourist attraction for health-conscious genteel travellers. The oldest and most fashionable resort of this kind in the region—and celebrated throughout Scotland—was the well at Moffat which was used from the 1650s onwards. Merely the well-shaft now survives, situated on the edge of a ravine (NT 092072); the well house, pavilion, and massive Hydropathic Hotel (1878-1921) have all gone, but in Moffat High Street the former Bath House, opened in 1827 and converted into the Town Hall in 1897, is tangible reminder of the time when the mineral waters were piped to the town from the upper spring at the well.

Moffat Town Hall, formerly Bath House

Finally, a word about the descriptive value judgements used in this book. As the late Sir John Betjeman pointed out in 'Antiquarian Prejudice' (*First and Last Loves*, 1952), it is almost impossible for the writer of a guide to support his subject at length without occasional recourse to a limited stock of epithets: attractive, beautiful, charming, fascinating, fine, impressive, interesting, picturesque, significant, splendid, etc. Such descriptions are unavoidable, but the visual qualities of the photographs and the monuments most often speak better for themselves. The emphasis here is on those aspects which are measurable according to a national standard of antiquity, size, rarity, and geographical distribution, in order to place the monuments of this region in a wider perspective. In terms of historic buildings and monuments, Dumfries and Galloway may not quite have everything, but many of its antiquities stand high in their respective national league tables. Every resident knows, and every visitor will find out, what—in the best possible sense—a fascinating region this is!

**Kenmure Castle
in an engraving
of around 1800**

EXCURSIONS

The following excursions are selected to show the density and variety of monuments that can be seen in different parts of the region. Each of the circuits can be completed within a day, but they are better done in easy stages. The actual time taken, and the degree to which each site is explored at first visit, will vary according to circumstances, weather, and taste. The journeys are centred upon historic towns with museums, to which the visitor can have recourse; two excursions start from Kirkcudbright and three from Dumfries, both towns meriting day-long tours in their own right. Visitors to Stranraer and western Galloway may wish to explore some of the monuments in neighbouring south Ayrshire which are described in the companion guide to *Glasgow, Clydeside and Stirling*.

The densest clusters of visitable sites, and hence most of the tours, are located in the river valleys and coastal areas. For the uplands, the visitor travelling by car will be able to arrange his own itineraries with little difficulty, and serious walkers will find that the route of the Southern Upland Way runs close to a number of monuments mentioned or described in this guide (eg from west to east, nos 1, 64, 15, 26, 28, 89, 19, 16, 9). Away from the major trunk routes, many of the country roads of Dumfries and Galloway, especially those of the Machars and around Kirkcudbright, are a cyclist's delight.

KEY	
Bridge	⌒
Broch, dun, fort	○
Castle	♖
Church	♱
Cross, cross-slab	▮
Cupmarks	◉
Harbour	⚓
House, rural building	■
Industrial Monument	▮
Lighthouse	♟
Long Cairn	⬭
Military Monument	✖
Miscellaneous later monument	▽
Miscellaneous prehistoric	⣿
Moated Site	◡
Monument	●
Motte	⌂
Roman Monument	☐
Standing Stone	▲
Stone Circle	⦂
Town, village	●
Town *explored in text*	◉

Orchardton Castle

THE RHINS

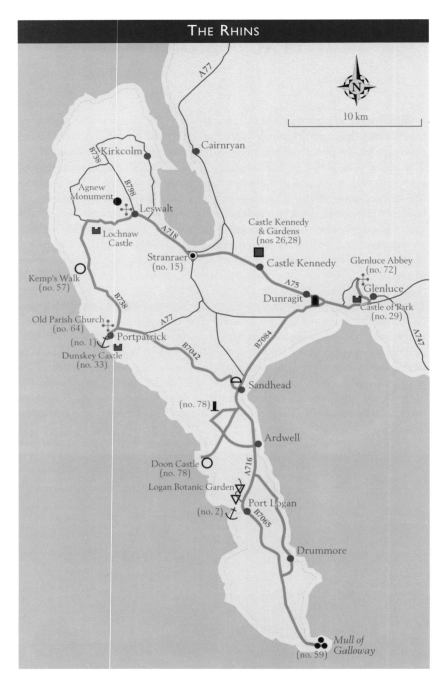

From Stranraer the A 75 goes east taking the traveller past the gates of Castle Kennedy (nos 26, 28) and the former creamery at Dunragit (NX 153573). At Glenluce there are branch-roads leading to Glenluce Abbey (no. 72) and Castle of Park (no. 29). Return along the A 75 and the A 715, skirting the head of Luce Bay, a productive source of much archaeological material and now a Ministry of Defence area with restricted access. After joining the A 716 observe the dominant motte at Balgreggan (NX 096505), which forms part of the cliff-terrace above the old raised beach. South of Sandhead, follow the signposts to Kirkmadrine (no. 78) and back again, directly to the A 716 or indirectly along the by-ways to Ardwell; the route to 'Doon Castle' (no. 53), incidentally, begins at the cross-roads at Clachanmore. Beyond Ardwell take the right fork to Port Logan to see the harbour (no. 2), the fish pond (NX 096413) and Logan Botanic Garden, which originated in its present form in about 1900, created out of a conventional walled vegetable garden for Logan House and incorporating a fragment of Balzieland Castle (NX 095426).

Former town house (now museum), Stranraer

Before returning, the visitor should consider a trip to the Mull of Galloway (no. 59), if an hour can be spared. Then northwards along the A 716, the conventional route to Portpatrick is via the B 7042 from the junction between Sandhead and Balgreggan motte. The harbour (no. 1), church (no. 64), and Dunskey Castle (no. 33) are Portpatrick's principal historic attractions, but note also the railway archaeology and the hotel. The road northwards from Portpatrick goes past the track down to 'Kemp's Walk' fort (no. 57); Lochnaw Castle (NW 991628, open to visitors) is the oldest inhabited house in western Galloway. Follow the B 7043 into Leswalt, the centre of the medieval parish which still embraces half of Stranraer. The old church lies towards the west end of the village at NX 015638; its 1828 successor stands at the crossroads at the eastern end. To the north-west is the Agnew Monument which is a prominent landmark.

Glenluce Abbey: chapter house interior

**Portpatrick
from the air**

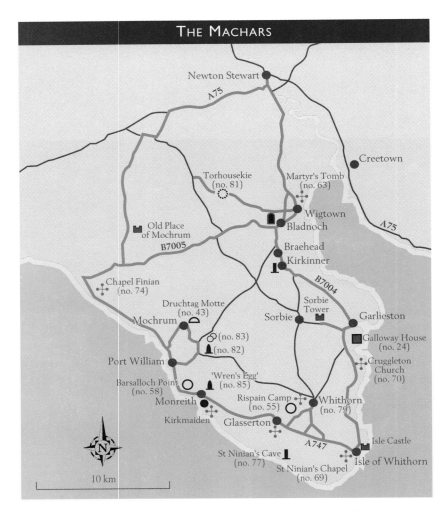

Begin at either Newton Stewart or Wigtown (no. 63) and make the journey on the B 733 to the stone circle at Torhousekie (no. 81). Back on the main road (A 714), note the distillery at Bladnoch (NX 420542; founded 1817, enlarged 1878), and follow the A 746 through Kirkinner where the church contains an Anglian cross. Take the B 7004 fork to Garlieston and Galloway House (no. 24); a short distance to the west, off the B 7052, is Sorbie Tower (NX 451471), a large L-plan tower-house consolidated by the Clan Hannay Society. Return to the B 7004 and the B 7063 past Cruggleton Church (no. 70) to Isle of Whithorn and St Ninian's Chapel (no. 69). To the north of the village main street is Isle Castle (NX 476365), a three-storeyed tower dating from 1674.

The A 750 takes the modern pilgrim from the village-port to Whithorn (no. 79), where inspection of the excavation sites and the stones in the museum is an essential prelude to a visit to St Ninian's Cave (no. 77). Return along the A 750 and take the minor branch across the A 747 to Physgill and the car park at Kidsdale Farm, whence there is a 1.8 km walk to the cave. Nearby, off the A 747 and A 746 respectively, Glasserton Church (NX 421380) and Rispain Camp (no. 55) provide a local break in the

Whithorn
Museum: the
Petrus stone

Ninianic theme, the developed architecture of the church reflecting the patronage of the Earls of Galloway and their descendants (see no. 24) and its tower one of the rare Scottish products of the architect, JB Papworth (see no. 23).

Continue along the A 747 in the direction of Monreith; just before the village a branch to the left leads down to Kirkmaiden churchyard (NX 365399) past a rock outcrop on the headland bearing cup-and-ring markings (NX 364402) and a sculptured bronze otter, a fitting monument to Gavin Maxwell (d. 1969). A right fork in Monreith village leads to the track to Blairbuie Farm and the 'Wren's Egg' (no. 85). The A 747 follows the coastline below Barsalloch fort (no. 58); at Port William turn inland on the A 714 to see the cups-and-rings and standing stones at Drumtroddan (nos 82, 83). From the A 714 west of Drumtroddan take the series of minor roads to Mochrum village and the motte of Druchtag (no. 43), returning thence to the coast and on to Chapel Finian (no. 74). Return to Wigtown on the B 7005, from which a minor road branches northwards across a watery moorland to Kirkcowan, and ultimately Newton Stewart. On the east side beyond the northern end of Mochrum Loch obtain a glimpse through the trees of the remarkable double-towered Old Place of Mochrum (NX 308541).

Garlieston

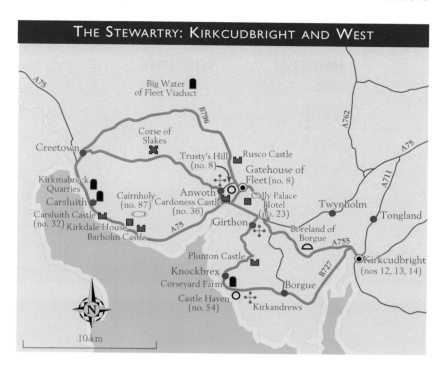

THE STEWARTRY: KIRKCUDBRIGHT AND WEST

Depart from Kirkcudbright across the bridge on the A 755. Further west at Boreland of Borgue its route runs fairly close to a well-preserved motte (NX 646517) which has a historical context. Follow the main roads into Gatehouse of Fleet (no. 8), whose surroundings include Cally Palace Hotel (no. 23), 'Trusty's Hill' (no. 46), Cardoness Castle (no. 36), and Anwoth Old Church (NX 582562). Further west on the A 75 is the signpost to Cairnholy chambered cairns (no. 87); also standing on the hillside above the main road are Kirkdale House (NX 515533) and Barholm Castle (NX 520529), a reasonably complete late 16th-century tower-house. Further on, Carsluith Castle (no. 32) is an obvious wayside feature on the A 75. The salmon stake-nets in the river estuary and the little smokehouse at Carsluith are witness to fishing industries, whilst the great quarries at Kirkmabreck (NX 4856) and the building materials of Creetown itself demonstrate the local impact of granite quarrying.

From Creetown, which has a Gem Rock Museum in the old school, the return journey can be made either on the old military road over the Corse of Slakes, or in a wider loop which follows the former course of the railway before descending the valley of the Water of Fleet past the late 15th-century Rusco Castle (NX 584604; Fleet Valley National Scenic Area).

From Gatehouse follow the succession of minor roads which provide an opportunity for seeing or visiting the old church at Girthon (NX 605533), 16th-century Plunton Castle (NX 605507), the remarkable early 20th-century farmstead at Corseyard (NX 591485), the dun at Castle Haven (no. 54), the churchyard at Kirkandrews (NX 600481), and Borgue village. Return to Kirkcudbright on the B 727.

**Gatehouse
of Fleet:
cotton mills,
c 1847**

**Cairnholy II
chambered cairn**

Cardoness Castle

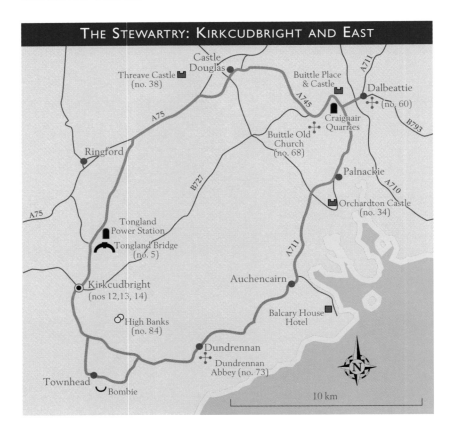

Travel north from Kirkcudbright on the A 711 over Tongland Bridge (no. 5) and past the principal control station of the Galloway Hydro-Electric Scheme (NX 695536). Join the A 75, and just west of Castle Douglas follow the signposts northwards to Threave Castle (no. 38) by car, foot, and ferry. Return to the A 75, and at the northern end of Castle Douglas take the Dalbeattie Road (A 745) to Buittle Old Church (no. 68). The road twists down into the valley of the Urr above Buittle Place and Castle (NX 819616); Craignair Quarries, set into the hillside, are the source of much Dalbeattie granite. Continue southwards on the A 711, and south of Palnackie take the left turn to Orchardton Castle (no. 34). At Auchencairn branch left again to visit Balcary House Hotel (NX 823495), a former haunt of smugglers. From Auchencairn the A 711 leads directly to Kirkcudbright past Dundrennan Abbey (no. 73). A longer homeward route from Dundrennan goes by a series of minor roads over the hills past the moated site at Bombie (NX 707501). Time may permit a visit to the cup-and-ring markings at High Banks (no. 84).

Threave Castle

**Dundrennan
Abbey**

**MacLellan's
Castle,
Kirkcudbright**

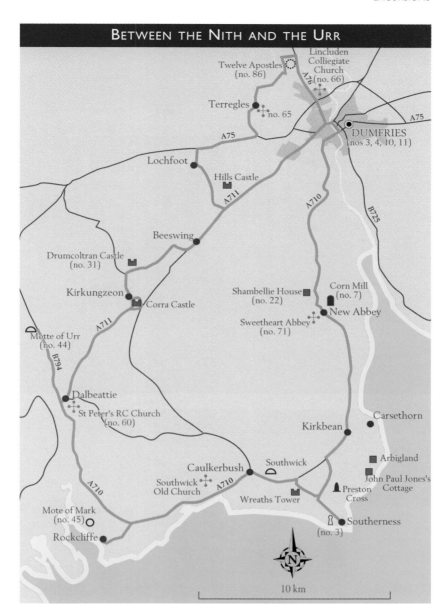

BETWEEN THE NITH AND THE URR

Lincluden
Colliegiate
Church
(no. 66)

Twelve Apostles
(no. 86)

A76

Terregles
no. 65

A75

DUMFRIES
(nos 3, 4, 10, 11)

A75

Lochfoot

Hills Castle

A711

A710

B725

Beeswing

Drumcoltran Castle
(no. 31)

Shambellie House
(no. 22)

Corn Mill
(no. 7)

Kirkungzeon

Corra Castle

New Abbey

Sweetheart Abbey
(no. 71)

A711

Motte of Urr
(no. 44)

B794

Dalbeattie

St Peter's RC Church
(no. 60)

Carsethorn

Kirkbean

Arbigland

Caulkerbush

Southwick

John Paul Jones's
Cottage

Southwick
Old Church

A710

Preston
Cross

Wreaths Tower

Mote of Mark
(no. 45)

A710

Southerness
(no. 3)

Rockcliffe

N

10 km

Begin in Dumfries and take the Solway Coast road (A 710) to New Abbey
(Nith Estuary National Scenic Area), where Shambellie (no. 22), the Corn
Mill (no. 7), Sweetheart Abbey (no. 71), and the village itself are worth at
least half a day. Continue along the A 710, past the entrance to Arbigland
(NX 989574; an 18th-century house whose gardens are sometimes open to
visitors, and contain the reputed cottage birthplace of John Paul Jones).
A diversion to see Southerness Lighthouse (no. 3) runs near to Preston
Cross (NX 969564), and returns past the stump of Wreaths Tower
(NX 952565). Pass through Southwick on the A 710 (East Stewartry Coast
National Scenic Area) with the Home Farm on the south side, and a worn-
looking motte (NX 936570) above the road. Further west beyond
Caulkerbush, a short drive into the hills leads to the old parish church of

**Corn Mill,
New Abbey:
gears cupboard**

**Sweetheart
Abbey**

Southwick, a much-altered medieval ruin whose tombstones are perhaps of greater interest than the church itself. The next diversion from the A 710 is at Colvend, turning left down to Rockcliffe for the Mote of Mark (no. 45).

At the crossroads in Dalbeattie proceed straight ahead on the B 794, and about 4 km further north is the Motte of Urr (no. 44). Return to Dalbeattie, turn left on to the A 711 past St Peter's RC Church (no. 60), and, noting all the shiny grey granite hereabouts, continue as far as the Kirkgunzeon turn-off (the ruins of Corra Castle stand on the north side of the A 711 just beyond the junction). Follow the minor roads through Kirkgunzeon village and on to Drumcoltran Castle (no. 31). Return to the A 711 at Beeswing, and then either directly back to Dumfries, or turn left at Lochanhead on a minor road past the approach to Hills Castle (NX 912726) to join the A 75. A short distance further east there is a choice of minor roads across the Cargen Water to Terregles and its church (no. 65), and then on to New Bridge and the 'Twelve Apostles' stone circle (no. 86). The return to Dumfries on the A 76 goes past the road to Lincluden Collegiate Church (no. 66).

Motte of Urr

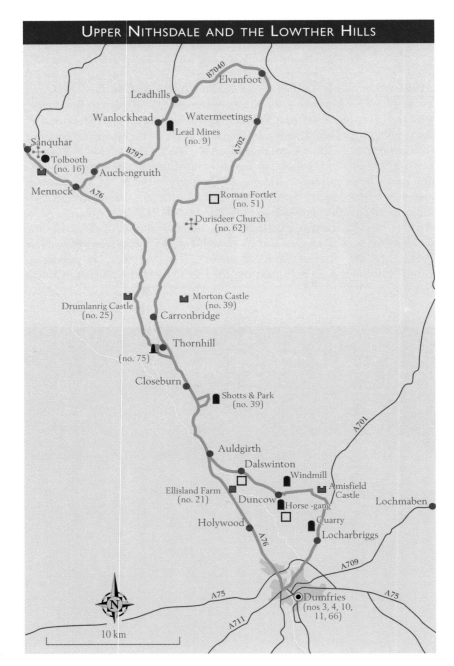

UPPER NITHSDALE AND THE LOWTHER HILLS

From Dumfries take the A 76 northwards to Ellisland Farm (no. 21), and then past neighbouring Friars' Carse on to Thornhill where a short westward diversion leads across Nith Bridge on the A 702 to the cross-shaft (no. 75). Further north, Drumlanrig Castle (no. 25) constitutes a major objective, and then onwards up the Nith Valley to Sanquhar to see the town house (no. 16), the castle (NS 785092), and the effigy in the church (NS 779102). Return to Mennock and turn left on to the B 797 which pursues a narrow winding course through the Lowther Hills to Wanlockhead (no. 9).

Durisdeer
Church:
headstone
commemorating
the children of
William Lukup,
master mason

A return journey via Leadhills and Elvanfoot on the B 7040 and A 702 makes a convenient circuit past Durisdeer where the church (no. 62) is a fitting complement to Drumlanrig. Those with time and energy to spare may wish to make the expedition on foot to the Roman fortlet (no. 51) and the Well Path. Further south, Morton Castle (no. 39) makes a rewarding digression from the A 702.

After re-joining the A 76 there are options for eastward diversions below Closeburn to examine the Garroch waterpower system at Shotts and Park (NX 907913), and then at Auldgirth where a minor road continues on the left bank of the Nith through Dalswinton and Kirkton. From aerial photographs Dalswinton (NX 933849) is known to have been the site of a huge Agricolan Roman fort which was destroyed and subsequently replaced by a cavalry fort downstream at Carzield (NX 969818). Other tempting diversions on this last stage of the journey include the windmill tower at Duncow (NX 974838), Amisfield Castle (NX 992838), the sandstone quarry at Locharbriggs (NX 987813), and the horse-gang at West Gallaberry (NX 964826).

**Distant view
of Drumlanrig
Castle**

**Water-bucket
pumping engine,
Wanlockhead**

Morton Castle

Amisfield Tower

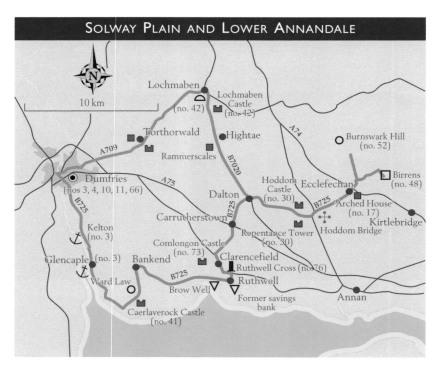

SOLWAY PLAIN AND LOWER ANNANDALE

Lochmaben
Lochmaben (no. 42)
Lochmaben Castle (no. 42)
10 km
Torthorwald
Hightae
A74
Burnswark Hill (no. 52)
A709
Rammerscales
B7020
Birrens (no. 48)
Dumfries (nos 3, 4, 10, 11, 66)
A75
Hoddom Castle (no. 30)
Ecclefechan
B725
'Arched House' (no. 17)
Dalton
B725
Kirtlebridge
Kelton (no. 3)
Carrutherstown
Repentance Tower (no. 30)
Hoddom Bridge
Comlongon Castle (no. 73)
Glencaple (no. 3)
Bankend
Clarencefield
Ruthwell Cross (no. 76)
Ward Law
B725
Brow Well
Ruthwell
Former savings bank
Annan
Caerlaverock Castle (no. 41)

Head south from Dumfries on the B 725 past St Michael's Church (no. 61) and the grave of Robert Burns, and the Crichton Royal Infirmary. This road joins the left bank of the Nith through Kelton and Glencaple, one-time trading centres of the Port of Dumfries (no. 3). Follow the route past the salt marsh on to Caerlaverock Castle (no. 41), noting its low-lying position in relation to earlier fortifications on Ward Law to the north. Continue on the

Caerlaverock Castle

B 725 over the Lochar Water at Bankhead, and past the restored Brow Well (NY 085675), where the mortally ill Robert Burns tried to cure himself in 1796. At the junction with the B 724 turn right to visit the building at the east end of Ruthwell village which was the first-ever commercial savings bank (1810); then collect the key for Ruthwell Church and its magnificent cross (no. 76), returning through Clarencefield to visit Comlongon Castle (no. 37).

Continue on the B 725, across the A 75, and on to Dalton (NY 115740), a small agricultural village whose early 18th-century church incorporates medieval remains. Stay on the B 725 for Hoddom Castle, Repentance Tower (no. 30), the old churchyard and Early Christian site at Hoddom Bridge (NY 166726), and on to Ecclefechan for Carlyle's Birthplace (no. 17). Further on, at Middlebie, a branch to the south leads to Birrens Roman fort (no. 48); return thence along the B 725 and turn to the north before reaching Ecclefechan in order to take a closer look at Burnswark Hill (no. 52).

Back at Dalton, follow the B 7020 past Hightae, largest of the Royal Four Towns of Lochmaben; to the west, Rammerscales (NY 088776; 1773) is a Georgian house which is sometimes open to visitors. About 1.5 km south of Lochmaben a signposted track leads to the later of the two castles (no. 42) which lies within the area of a Nature Reserve. From Lochmaben take the A 709 west to Dumfries through Torthorwald (no. 18) and across the drained Lochar Moss.

**Dumfries,
Dervorguilla
Bridge**

**Comlongon
Castle and House**

Ruthwell Cross

TRANSPORT AND COMMUNICATIONS

Portpatrick Harbour by William Daniell, 1816

A long coastline bordering the Solway Firth, the Irish Sea and the North Channel gives much of Galloway a strong and attractive maritime character. One cannot over-emphasise the importance of sea transport that has linked the province with north-west England, the Isle of Man, Ireland, the rest of western Scotland, and even abroad. The fact that the North Channel opposite the Rhins of Galloway provides the shortest sea-crossing (32 km) between Britain and Ireland remains crucial to the present-day transport network, and makes Stranraer a busy modern port. All around the coasts there are many small harbours of 18th- and 19th-century date still in use, mainly for pleasure craft, while places like Kirkcudbright and Garlieston (NX 4746) also manage to retain a traditional sea-faring atmosphere. However, it now requires an effort of imagination to appreciate that the Rivers Urr and Nith, as far upstream as Dalbeattie and Dumfries (no. 3), were once busy with water-borne commerce.

Although relatively sheltered, most of the Solway ports face the hazards of unusually high tides, strong currents and shifting sand-bars. Those of the more rugged and exposed western coast of the Rhins have occasionally felt the full blast of North Atlantic gales. There can be no more telling monument to the sheer destructive force of the sea than the wrecked remains of the outer harbour at Portpatrick (no. 1), nor a more poignant reminder of this power than the simple rubble monument in Agnew Park,

Stranraer (NX 055611). It commemorates those 133 persons who lost their lives in the sinking of the Stranraer-Larne ferry, 'Princess Victoria', during the exceptionally severe storm of 31 January/1 February 1953. Loch Ryan itself, however, is a safe haven, and was the scene of great activity in the Second World War: Cairnryan (NX 0668) was reconstructed as a military port to handle vital trans-Atlantic traffic, whilst a seaplane base at Wig Bay (NX 0367) on the opposite shore was host to the massive Sunderland flying-boats. Vestiges of these installations are still visible.

'Princess Victoria'
Monument,
Agnew Park,
Stranraer

Although nowhere matching the boldness and grandeur of some of the lighthouses of the western and northern seaboards, Galloway's coastal aids to navigation are of an unusual variety and antiquity. The circular church-tower at Portpatrick (no. 64), which dates from the 1620s, was almost certainly intended as a sea-mark for guiding boats into the harbour. The nucleus of Southerness Lighthouse (no. 3) was built in 1748, and is the second oldest surviving purpose-built lighthouse in the country. The stocky little light-tower on the pier at Port Logan (no. 2) looks much older than it actually is, but that does not detract from its interest and idiosyncratic charm. Corsewall Lighthouse (NW 980726), one of a trio of functioning lights on the Rhins, went into operation in November 1816, and was the first of the Northern Lighthouse Board's towers in southern Scotland. Mull of Galloway (NX 156304) was lighted in 1830, and Killantringan (NW 981564) in 1900.

With its tidal rivers and numerous creeks and bays, the much-indented Solway coastline was ideally suited for contraband trade, especially with the Isle of Man which until 1876 lay outside British Customs regulations. The smuggling traditions of the area have been vividly brought to life by episodes in Sir Walter Scott's *Guy Mannering* and S R Crockett's *The Raiders* which is set on a fictionalised version of Hestan Island (NX 8350). The coast abounds with landing-places and caves allegedly associated with smuggling, and there are plenty of placenames indicative of the practice. Dirk Hatteraick's Cave (NX 518526; access very narrow and dangerous), about 200 m east of the mouth of the Kirkdale Burn, derives its name from the smuggler in *Guy Mannering*, but its stone-built recesses were probably nesting-boxes for pigeons, not bins for illicit goods. On the other hand, excavations in Torrs Cave (NX 676445) revealed 18th-century occupation-levels, probably relating to use by contraband traders. The archaeology of Solway smuggling is perhaps most audaciously represented by the storage vault in the basement of what is now the Balcary House Hotel (NX 823495). Overlooking a safe anchorage that was a much-frequented haunt of smugglers, the nucleus of the present house was built in the 18th century by a Manx company (Clark, Grain and Quirk); they were evidently prepared to conduct their nefarious business without making great efforts at its concealment.

'Smugglers Solway Firth' by Frank Short c 1894

Portpatrick Harbour

1 Portpatrick Harbour

18th and 19th centuries AD.

NW 9954.

In the days of sail, Portpatrick was the usual Scottish terminal on the short sea-crossing between Galloway and Ulster. Such journeys had probably been made since time immemorial, but it was largely through the efforts of a cross-channel landlord in the first half of the 17th century that Portpatrick and its Irish counterpart, Donaghadee, were able to convert their geographical advantages into exclusive privileges. Hugh Montgomery, lord of Ards, and from 1608 until his death in 1636, laird of Dunskey (including what was then known as Port Montgomery), acquired in 1616 a royal warrant restricting travel between Galloway and Ards to these two ports, making this a major route to the Scottish plantation of Ulster. Portpatrick was the main port of entry for imported Irish cattle, and from 1662 to 1848 was the principal station for the Irish ferry and packet-service. Upon the completion of the military road in 1765, it served as a transit-station for troops, a function commemorated by such names as Barrack Street and Colonel Street, and from 1790 was the terminus of a daily mail-coach service. Just as Gretna did for the English at the other end of this road, so Portpatrick enabled fugitive Irish couples to contract hurried marriages in accordance with Scottish procedures.

The early use of the landing-places here was assisted by few engineered works, and has left no obvious trace. Even the 'footprint' stone from which St Patrick made his mighty legendary stride across the North Channel was obliterated in the course of 19th-century harbour-works. A traveller in 1636 complained that it was a 'most craggy, filthy passage, ... very dangerous for horses to go in and out ...; and when any horses land here, they are thrown into the sea, and swim out'. In 1768 John Smeaton concluded that, except for a passenger landing-platform, the harbour was 'almost in a state of nature'. Because of the rocky inlet's natural limitations as a safe, sheltered and spacious anchorage, Portpatrick's potential as a major packet-station continually excited sharp differences of opinion, a point which rivals were never slow to pursue in their promotion of the claims of Port Logan, and subsequently Stranraer.

The harbour-works completed in 1778 in accordance with Smeaton's plan were the first in a century-long campaign to convert these limited facilities into a reliable major harbour. Smeaton's scheme to protect the rebuilt inner or northern harbour (which then lay around the rocky islet known as McCook's Craig) was nullified by the inadequacy of its northern pier and bulwark, twice rebuilt before their final destruction in 1801. This left only a south harbour with a lighthouse and a short pier which William Daniell illustrated in 1816, and of which a fragmentary stump still survives just north of the present late 19th-century lighthouse. This was the position when Telford made his unfavourable report in 1802, and these were some of the problems to which John Rennie addressed himself in 1814-18.

Rennie's plan was essentially a scaled-up version of Smeaton's scheme, involving much more massive and expensive piers. Work began in 1820; the south pier was completed in 1832, and the lighthouse at the pier-head in 1836. However, when this new pier was seriously breached by a hurricane in 1839, the north pier was left unfinished, as it remains to this day. Despite all these setbacks, a boat dock was built in 1865 to accommodate large mail-steamers and to connect with the railway. But Portpatrick's fate had already been sealed by the ability of steamboats, introduced by the Post Office in 1825, to make use of the sheltered waters of Loch Ryan. By the 1860s the Irish mails were being handled through Stranraer and Larne, and in 1868 the ferry service was officially transferred to that route. So far as Portpatrick was concerned, the final act of this epic struggle was the dismantling of the lighthouse at the south pier-head in 1871, and then, in 1873, the official abandonment of the outer harbour to the mercies of an unrelenting sea.

2 Port Logan Harbour

AD 1818-20.

NX 094405. At the W end of the seafront village.

Being the only comparatively safe natural anchorage on this exposed western coast, Port Logan or Port Nessock, as it is sometimes known, was a serious rival to Portpatrick as a possible terminal for Irish traffic. Efforts on the part of the McDouall owners to develop a harbour here were first recorded in 1682, but the existing remains correspond with the chief proposals made by John Rennie in a report of 1813. These were put into effect between 1818 and 1820 at the expense of Colonel Andrew McDouall of Logan. It was even intended to have an offshore breakwater covering the whole bay, but this, and the hopes for the harbour, were never realised. For a few decades Port Logan was used for a trade in Irish cattle and

local produce, but it was unable to oust Portpatrick when this in turn was being overtaken by Stranraer.

Even today, the Port Logan jetty is an impressive witness to its builder's ambitions. It extends in a broad arc some 185 m into the bay, and is constructed of large stone blocks. At the pier-head there is a sturdily- built lighthouse-tower with a stone-slabbed conical roof. The light-chamber has had wooden-framed windows and was reached by a ladder from the first floor, but there is no clear evidence of the actual method of lighting. A latrine with a mural chute was contrived under the outside stair. There are a few granite bollards, and the projecting socketed stones on the face of the inner quayside were designed to clasp upright wooden fenders.

3 Port of Dumfries

18th and 19th centuries AD.

NX 9754-NX 9676. In Dumfries on the left bank of the river at Whitesands and Dockhead; the lighthouse at Southerness is on the shore immediately beyond the end of the unclassified road through the village.

Although Dumfries had enjoyed the benefits of coastal and foreign trade since the Middle Ages, the volume of that trade, including links with the Baltic and the North American colonies, began to increase dramatically from the later 17th century onwards. However, the Nith, aptly described by Ian Donnachie as 'the most fickle of all rivers', remained the main channel of the town's commerce. Navigation for large vessels was hindered by the vagaries of tides, treacherous sandbanks and the shifting course of the river, particularly at its estuary, and throughout the 18th and 19th centuries the merchant burgesses of Dumfries made valiant efforts to overcome these difficulties. The Nith Navigation Commission, which was formed in 1811, straightened, deepened, and embanked the river channel in accordance with a scheme proposed by James Hollinsworth, engineer, but the labour of further improvement was required in 1836-40. Trade reached a peak in the mid-1840s, repaying the effort but not all the debts. The arrival of the railway in Dumfries in 1850 signalled the beginning of the long demise of the port, although there was a brief revival of seaborne trade in the two decades before 1914.

Port Logan Harbour (Left)

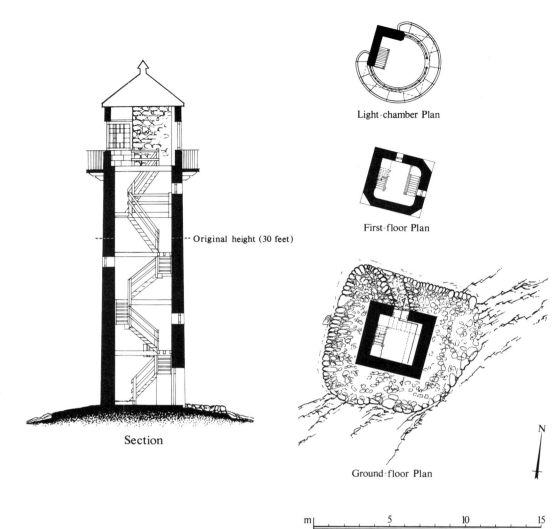

Light-chamber Plan

First-floor Plan

···· Original height (30 feet)

Ground-floor Plan

**Southerness
Lighthouse,
plans and section**

Section

**Southerness
Lighthouse**

As a registration authority, the port of Dumfries extended eastwards as far as the Sark, including Annan and five main quays on the Nith: Dockfoot (Dumfries), Castledykes, Kingholm, Laghall and Glencaple. At Carsethorn (NX 994598) there was a wooden pier built in about 1840 for the passenger steamship service to Liverpool. The quay at Dumfries now survives as the frontage of a riverside walk extending about 1 km downstream from the weir below the old bridge (no. 4) to Dockfoot Park and Castledykes (NX 9775). The major surviving harbour-works, however, are those at Kingholm (NX 974736) and at Glencaple (NX 994687). Both had quays that were built in 1746 and reconstructed in the early 19th century, Kingholm having a large boat dock scoured by a pair of conduits.

The most impressive testimony to the early efforts of the Dumfries traders is undoubtedly the square, rubble-built lighthouse-tower on the foreshore at Southerness (NX 977542), one of the earliest lighthouses in Scotland. It was intended to serve as a guide to ships in the exceedingly difficult waters of the Nith estuary and the inner Solway Firth. Originally built as a 9.1 m high beacon by Dumfries Town Council in 1748-9, it was heightened and altered in the 1780s and again in 1842-3. Lack of finance obliged the Nith Navigation Commission to extinguish the light in 1867. With a temporary revival of trade it was restored in 1894, and, raised to almost twice its original height, continued in active use until 1936. The lighthouse chamber and red sandstone upperworks date from this last restoration, and the brass frame of an 1894 lantern is mounted on the ruins of an old limekiln nearby. The interior, which is not normally accessible, contains no original features.

ROADS, TRACKS AND BRIDGES

The most ancient engineered roads in the province are those laid down by the Romans. They first entered Scotland in the Agricolan era in about AD 79, and developed their road network during the course of their intermittent occupation of southern Scotland. Their main western trunk route ran, much as today's A 74, from Carlisle and the fort at Stanwix on Hadrian's Wall northwards into Annandale and Upper Clydesdale. Near what is now Lockerbie, one road, probably of the Antonine period, about AD 140-163, appears to have branched north-eastwards up Dryfesdale to the remote fort at Raeburnfoot (no. 50), at the head of Eskdale, and onward to the major centre at Newstead near Melrose. Also from Lockerbie another road ran westwards to serve a chain of garrisons in Galloway and in Nithsdale which extended at least as far north as Sanquhar; near Durisdeer a road known later as the Well Path swung back north-eastwards to rejoin the main trunk route in Clydesdale. Not much is known of

**Military Road,
Corse of Slakes**

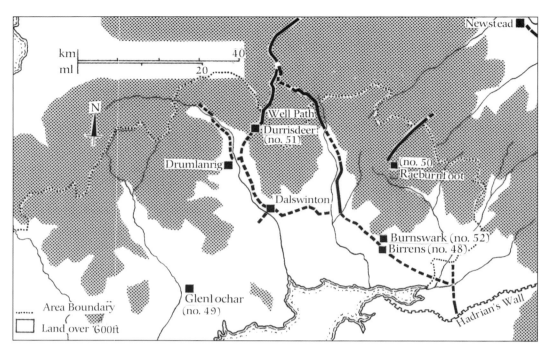

**Map showing
Roman roads
and sites**

the road(s) to the Galloway forts at Glenlochar and Gatehouse, nor of the direct route from the south through Eskdale to Newstead.

In the east there are visible traces of a Roman road south-west of the fort at Raeburnfoot (no. 50) between NT 237961 and 244977; it reappears at Mid Raeburn (NT 264005), 3.2 km north-east of the fort, and then crosses the hills to the regional boundary at Craik Cross (NT 303047) and beyond, an impressive 10.5 km stretch of ancient roadway. A 6 m-wide cambered surface with side-ditches has been carved out of the basic shale rock, and on sloping ground it has been artificially terraced. The Annandale road is best seen in its upland course between Coats Hill (NT 0704), west of Moffat, and the regional boundary at March Burn (NT 042138) where there may once have been a bridge. The road runs in characteristically straight lengths close to the ridge between the valleys of the Annan and the Evan Water. It varies in overall width between 4.5 m and 6.4 m, with metalled running surfaces about 0.46 m in depth. The quarry-pits, from which the broken stone was obtained, survive on either side of the road as small circular or oval scoops, many linked to the road with short ramps. The best-preserved section of the Nithsdale 'loop' is the grassy road known as the Well Path which makes a uniformly graded ascent of the narrow defile from

Durisdeer village (NS 894038) past the fortlet (no. 51) to the regional boundary at the watershed of the Potrail Water (NS 916060).

The Well Path, like many other Roman roads, witnessed regular use in medieval and later times. It formed part of one of the overland pilgrimage routes from central Scotland to the shrine of St Ninian at Whithorn, a journey which led thence through Penpont, St John's Town of Dalry and Minnigaff. A more southerly route went via Lochmaben, Dumfries and Tongland, whilst royal progress from Stirling was usually through Glasgow, Ayr and Glenluce. Despite the existence of a safe harbour at Isle of Whithorn, close to the shrine, the indications are that most pilgrims, obviously except those from the Isle of Man, travelled overland. King James IV (1488-1513) was for a time almost an annual visitor to Whithorn, and the records of his reign provide the best documented itineraries.

Tracing the evidence on the ground is another matter. Medieval highways over open moorland, like those used for droving cattle, generally comprised sets of alternative tracks, not a single clearly defined road. Parts of the track, marked on O.S. map as the 'Old Edinburgh Road', which climbs up out of Minnigaff and on to

Dervorguilla
Bridge, Dumfries
by Francis Grose,
1789

Clatteringshaws on a line generally north of the A712, are almost certainly medieval, whilst the 'Old Pack Road' which runs north-south across Dundeugh Forset south of Carsphairn also has a claim to antiquity. In the south, the major monument to medieval road transport is the old bridge across the Nith at Dumfries (no. 4).

Another set of medieval tracks crossed the upper reaches of the Solway Firth between England and Scotland. The most important of these crossing-points was the 'Sulwath', literally the 'muddy ford' which has given its name to the whole firth. It traversed the mouths of the Rivers Sark and Esk, linking with the Rockcliffe Marsh and the 'Stoneywath' across the Eden estuary. On the Scottish side the large granite boulder known as the Clochmabenstane (NY 312659), which became a recognised place of assembly on the western March, stands near the mouth of the Kirtle Water and the northern end of the ford. On the southern shore there is the lonely monument to King Edward I of England, who was one of the more fearsome users of the Solway and who died there in 1307 encamped on Burgh Marsh. This ford was a regular military route, and it is no coincidence that its northern hinterland became a battleground in,

for example, 1297, 1449 and 1542. As readers of *Redgauntlet* will recall, the crossing itself could be a battle against the treachery of both sands and tides. King Alexander II of Scotland is reputed to have lost as many as 1,900 men to the onrushing waters of Eden in the passage here in 1216.

Statute Labour and the County Commissioners of Supply provided a means of improving the roads from the 1660s onwards, but the first big modern road-building programme was that undertaken by the military, mainly in 1763-5. Although, in the aftermath of the Jacobite rebellions, the government devoted most of its attention in Scotland to the opening up of the Highlands, the longest single stretch of military road constructed in this period was in fact the 169 km route across Dumfries and Galloway from Bridge of Sark to Portpatrick. Its main purpose was to 'open a speedy, and certain communication between Great Britain and Ireland, especially with regard to the passage of troops from one kingdom to another whenever the exigency of affairs may require it.' The work mostly involved the reconstruction and realignment of existing routes with the provision of new bridges. A 25.7 km coastal spur to Ballantrae was added in 1780-2.

Dervorguilla Bridge, Dumfries

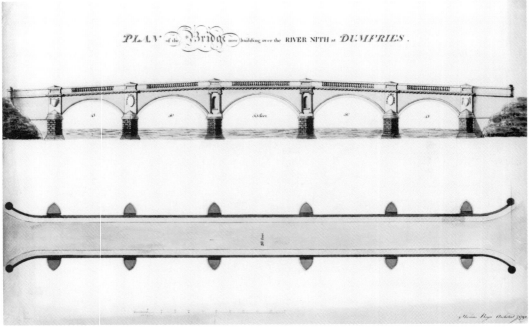

Buccleuch Street Bridge, Dumfries: design drawing, 1792

Today, parts of the A75 and minor roads in its vicinity mark the line of the main military route; its final stage from Stranraer went by Crailloch and Knockglass (NX 0358) on the more direct 'Old Portpatrick Road'. Elsewhere, the character of the old road can best be appreciated by walking the stretch from Black Park (NX 382646) to NX 353633, and more especially the Corse of Slakes road between Anwoth, King's Laggan and Creetown. Here, the hilly terrain had presented engineering problems and conditions similar to those encountered in the Highlands. This section of the road was often impassable in winter, and was abandoned as a main thoroughfare upon the completion of the coastal route between Gatehouse and Creetown in 1790. Thus, an unmetalled 4.8 km length of the old road between Anwoth (NX 582562) and Glen (NX 548582) now makes a very pleasant walk through delightful countryside, and includes one of the hairpin bends so characteristic of the military road-builders.

The Turnpikes Act of the 1790s ushered in a new era of toll-funded road building, whose major monuments are a series of outstanding bridges: the Buccleuch Street Bridge at Dumfries (no. 4); the Tongland Bridge (no. 5); Cree Bridge, Newton Stewart (NX 411656; John Rennie, engineer, 1814); and Ken Bridge, New Galloway (NX 640783; John Rennie, 1822). Historically, the unobtrusive little footbridge (no. 6) over the River Esk at Langholm is even more significant. Dating from 1813, it has the distinction of being the oldest surviving arched iron bridge in Scotland. For Eskdale, the honour is especially appropriate because Thomas Telford (1757-1834), one of the greatest civil engineers the world has ever known, was born at the remote hamlet of Glendinning in the hills to the north-west. He began his career as a journeyman mason in Langholm where he assisted in the building of the three-arched bridge over the Esk (NY 363848).

---

4 Dumfries, Bridges

15th century; late 18th century AD.

NX 968760, 968761. At Whitesands; the old bridge, now a footbridge, is a convenient means of reaching the museum from the town centre.

With its six arches and solid piers built in local red sandstone the old bridge over the Nith at Dumfries is a picturesque and memorable sight; it is also the oldest surviving multiple-arched stone bridge in Scotland, second only to the single-arched Bridge of Balgownie at Aberdeen in point of antiquity. Known as Dervorguilla Bridge, it has obviously inherited the name of its late 13th-century and probably timber-built predecessor. However, its construction was funded, not by the munificent Dervorguilla de Balliol but by the Douglases and the Burgh of Dumfries, and building work is known

to have been in progress in 1431. The bridge was half wrecked by floods in 1620, and evidence of rebuilding can be detected in the eastern half of the structure. In fact, the bridge had no less than nine arches until the early 19th century when it lost its three easternmost arches and became restricted to foot traffic, hence the somewhat abrupt stepped approach. With its 3.9 m-wide carriageway and its arched toll-gate (removed in 1769), the old bridge had been equal to the demands of medieval wheeled traffic in and out of Galloway, but by the late 18th century its retirement had become long overdue.

The new bridge was a five-arched structure designed by Thomas Boyd, a local architect (see no. 21). The construction of the bridge involved an elaborate ramped approach along what is now Buccleuch Street, and problems were encountered in the laying of foundations on that bank. The bridge was finally completed in 1794, and almost exactly a century later, in 1893, it was widened and had pedestrian paths cantilevered out. Since then it has undergone two major overhauls, and now shares the town's considerable traffic load with St Michael's Bridge (1927) downstream.

---

5 Tongland Bridge

AD 1807/8.

NX 691533. Carries the A 711 across the River Dee.

Because it is shrouded by trees and has a level carriageway with no rise to the crown of the arch, this handsome and well-engineered bridge does not make its special qualities obvious to modern road-users. Indeed, the fact that it was the first bridge to have weight-saving hollow ribbed spandrels instead of a solid masonry arch is one of its technical accomplishments that remains completely invisible.

On a single arch of 34.1 m span, it crosses a steep-sided gorge at the uppermost reach of the Dee estuary where the river has a remarkable tidal rise of 6 m and more. The foundations laid in the first building season (1804) were almost immediately washed away, and work recommenced under new contractors in the following year, the bridge finally

Tongland Bridge: drawing in Telford Atlas, 1838

Tongland Bridge

being completed and opened in 1807/8. Designed by Thomas Telford in association with the celebrated Edinburgh architect and painter, Alexander Nasmyth, the bridge has a very striking appearance. The arch is flanked by rounded turrets which, together with the corbelled and battlemented parapets, convey a marked castellated effect. To assist the flow of water at high tides, each of the approaches is pierced by three tall and narrow pointed flood-arches.

6 Duchess Bridge, Langholm

AD 1813.

NY 355852. On the S bank the riverside walk can be approached across the playing fields from the B 709.

This footbridge, which can lay claim to being the oldest surviving cast-iron arched bridge in Scotland, forms part of a pleasant riverside walk on the northern outskirts of Langholm. It crosses the River Esk to serve Langholm Lodge, a former residence of the Dukes of Buccleuch, hence its name. It was designed by William Keir, Director of Works on the Buccleuch estate, and was built in 1813 with iron cast in Workington. It is now somewhat hidden by trees and no longer, as in 1835, the 'object of great attention to travellers as they enter the town by the north'. In construction it is closely comparable to the famous Telford-designed road bridge at Craigellachie (1814-15), albeit simpler and of a smaller scale. Its arch, which has a clear span of 30.7 m, is set within masonry abutments, and is made up of sectional arch ribs and transverse ribs of cast iron connected by interlocking dovetailed joints.

RAILWAYS

Two of the main Anglo-Scottish lines traverse Dumfriesshire *en route* to Glasgow: the former Caledonian Railway (1845-) runs from Gretna Junction via Lockerbie and Beattock, whilst the ex-Glasgow and South Western (1850) heads for Annan, Dumfries and Nithsdale. A stiff climb northwards from Beattock through the Lowther Hills into Clydesdale nowadays poses few problems for electric trains, but modernisation has involved the removal or alteration of old trackside features. At Quintinshill (NY 322693), a short distance north of Gretna, one can now only visualise the scene of the worst disaster in British railway history. On 22 May 1915 a multiple collision here claimed an estimated 227 lives, the majority of them from a troop train carrying the 7th Battalion of the Royal Scots on what was intended to be the first stage of their journey to Gallipoli.

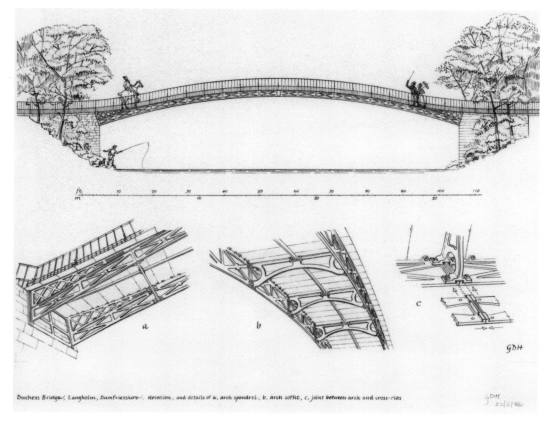

Duchess Bridge; Langholm, Dumfriesshire: elevation, and details of a, arch spandrel, b, arch soffit, c, joint between arch and cross-ribs

Duchess Bridge, Langholm: elevation and details (a) spandrel, (b) underside, (c) joint between arch and cross-ribs, by GD Hay

Annan (1848) and Dumfries (1859) on the former Glasgow and South Western route are the best of the few surviving stations in the region, stylishly built in red sandstone ashlar masonry with glazed platform awnings and contemporary details. Immediately south of Annan nothing except the landward embankments remains of the 1.6 km-long Solway viaduct (NY 2164; 1865/70-1935), which was built to assist the transport of haematite ore from Cumberland to the steelworks of Lanarkshire. Indeed, apart from the operational line between Ayr and Stranraer, railways are now a fading memory in the Galloway landscape.

The major monument of the old jointly operated Portpatrick Railway is the remote twenty-arch viaduct above the Big Water of Fleet (NX 5564; 1861), which has masonry piers encased in brick. At Portpatrick itself the site of the railway station (NX 003545; 1862-1950) is now a caravan park. However, the dramatic and steep approach from cliff-top cuttings near Dunskey Castle (no. 33) and remnants of the short reverse spur from the station to the harbour must give some holidaymakers a taste for railway archaeology, and a chance to re-create imaginatively the sights and sound of steam traction.

Railway viaduct over Big Water of Fleet

INDUSTRY 2

Corn Mill, New Abbey

Dumfries and Galloway has always been a predominantly agricultural region, and many of its historic industries have grown out of traditional farming pursuits. Outside the uplands, conditions are equally well suited to the management of livestock and crops, but since about 1850 advantage has been taken of its lush pastures and mild climate to concentrate on dairying. In this, the area has acquired considerable renown, and now contains one-third of all Scottish dairy herds. The modern dairy industry, however, mainly reflects the changes made since 1933 when the Scottish Milk Marketing Board was established. Modern large-scale creameries receive the raw milk direct from the farms, and take the place of small local creameries and farm-based butter- and cheese-makers. However, as at Dunragit (NX 153573), the buildings of some of the older country creameries still remain, as do the dairies and domestic cheese-lofts of the farmsteads. It is also very fitting that the first milking machine for use in dairies should have been the invention of a Stewartry farmer in about 1891.

Despite the dominance of dairy farming in modern times, it is not strange that cattle of the native Galloway breed are beef, not dairy animals. These hardy beasts are easiest to recognise in their distinctively 'belted' form, and now stand as a symbol of an earlier pattern of livestock farming. From 1666, when Irish cattle were restricted in their access to English markets, until the middle of the 19th century, the export of beef or store cattle to England, particularly eastern England, was the region's most important single industry. With programmes of selective livestock breeding and large-scale enclosure for high quality pasture, landowners like Sir David Dunbar of Baldoon became pioneers of Scottish agricultural improvement, a century ahead of much of the rest of the country. At Baldoon (NX 4253), he built a huge cattle-park in which he could over-winter no less than 1,000 head of cattle, an enclosure which in 1684 was described as 'the first, and, as it were, the mother of all the rest'. The Stair estate made similar provision at Castle Kennedy, and tenant farmers followed suit in the early 18th century. By 1726 Minnigaff parish was 'so enclosed and divided for the ... improvement of sheep and black cattle that the whole farmers of these grounds have considerable advantage'. The remains of early enclosures can still be detected in these areas, especially in the vicinity of tower-houses.

Another permanent reminder of this early enclosure movement is the form of stock-proof wall known throughout the country as the 'Galloway dyke'. Drystone built and about 0.81 m broad at base, these walls rise to a maximum height of 1.6 m, more usually 1.3 m: the lower two-thirds is of conventional double- faced construction with hearting and intermittent 'throughbands' laid cross-wise; the upper third, the specially distinctive feature, is a single thickness dyke of big rough stones with wide interstices and no pinnings, deliberately built in this manner to allow light to show through. It is this open effect which deters stock from attempting them. The sunk fence or 'Galloway hedge' is a conventional double dyke combined with a thorn hedge, used when the dyke runs across a slope. In the construction of the dyke, the hedge is rooted on the uphill side, and laid across the footings in order to allow it to grow up the downhill face. Both types of dyke can be seen throughout the Galloway landscape, but are particularly common in the central southern zone between Castle Douglas and Creetown.

Drove routes are another legacy of the cattle trade, but the passage of numerous and large herds across the province created its own problems. To protect the interests of landowners and farmers of adjacent grounds and to ensure that the best roads remained in a reasonable condition, droves in some areas (particularly between New Galloway and Dumfries) were restricted to certain routes carefully marked out by order of the Privy Council. Cattle markets, tanneries and slaughter-houses grew up around the main collecting points *en route*. By 1830 Dumfries had no less than nine tanneries; leather-working was an offshoot craft, and clog-making became a speciality of Bridgend. A clogmaker's shop in Friars' Vennel, Dumfries, was the last in the country. Another indirect memorial to droving traffic is the iron mileage panel of 1827 affixed to the end wall of the Dumfries Mid Steeple (no. 10). Among the destinations listed on the panel, Huntingdon 272 miles (437.7 km) away is, to the modern eye, quite unexpected. To the Galloway drover, on the other hand, it was a regular objective, for Huntingdon was a major tryst for eastern England, and most of the 20-30,000 head of cattle then being exported annually went to Norwich; there they were sold and fattened for the London market on a diet of Norfolk turnips.

In Dumfries and Galloway the abundance of potatoes sustained another stock-rearing industry of considerable importance: pig production. In the early 19th century, according to one authority, almost every cottager in

Galloway kept a pig, the farmers three or more, and the villages swarmed with them. In Dumfriesshire it was reckoned that the annual returns from this industry were then around £50,000. Many must have agreed with the writer who in 1832 enthused that 'we love nothing better on a winter day than to encounter, on the English or Annan road, a long array of carts, each and all piled tier above tier with defunct porkers'. Old bacon factories like that at Hayknowes (NY 172653) are today's silent memorials to these unfortunate beasts and the industry which surrounded them.

Mid Steeple, Dumfries: mileage panel

Sheep farming has always been a feature of the Glenkens, upper Annandale and Eskdale. This branch of farming came to have important ramifications as the old-established woollen cloth industry passed from domestic to fully mechanised factory-based production in the later 18th and 19th centuries. After 1810, large-scale hosiery manufacture was centred on Dumfries; the sizes of the tweed mills erected in and around the town from the 1840s onwards proclaim its regional dominance in that branch of the industry as well. In Langholm, now the region's wool capital, full-scale tweed manufacture did not grow out of handloom weaving traditions until after 1851, but its progress thenceforward is marked by a series of fine Victorian mills.

The shift from mixed to specialised pastoral farming has been mirrored in the decay of arable-related industries such as corn threshing and grain milling; in the fertile areas that remained under cultivation, modern technology has been applied to these operations. The Galloway countryside, long a grain-exporting district, is thus scattered with redundant grain mills and fixed farm threshing-units.

A survey carried out in 1968 reported that the farmstead at Blairbuie (NX 362420) contained what was then the best-preserved water-powered threshing mill in

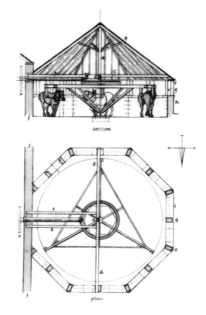

Horse-engine, West Gallaberry: plan and section by GD Hay

Galloway. At Shortrigg Farm, Hoddom (NY 162744), the tapered tower of a late 18th-century wind-powered threshing mill stands alongside the circular horse-engine house built after 1859 to supplement and then replace it. Very few threshers have survived, but, miraculously, the steading at West Gallaberry (NX 964826) has what may be the most complete surviving horse-engine mechanism in the country; within an octagonal shed it retains virtually all of its iron and wooden overhead draught-gear for three horses.

Grain mills were mostly water-powered, but the handful of windmills used for this purpose still catch the eye. Particularly conspicuous is the tower of the 1798 mill on Corberry Hill in Dumfries (NX 968758), which has been part of the town's museum for 150 years. At 13.3 m in height, the late 18th-century windmill tower at Mouswald Grange (NY 053736), which retains its adjacent corn-drying kiln, is the tallest in Scotland, whilst the stump of the vaulted tower mill at Logan (NX 116438) is among the oldest, dating from shortly before 1684.

A number of water-powered grain mills continued in operation until well into this century. One of the most complete is the corn mill (no. 7) in New Abbey village. It is Galloway's good fortune, and much to its credit, that this mill is the sole representative of the vertical-wheeled type in State custody on the Scottish mainland. Although occupying what is probably an ancient site, the existing mill, like the vast majority in Galloway, is of only 18th- and 19th-century date. But the great attraction of a mill of this kind, restored to working order, is not its antiquity, but the sight and sound of its moving parts, which have the same fascination as a powerful steam engine or the inside of a big clock.

Millwrights and blacksmiths kept the wheels turning, and makers of agricultural machinery found plenty of markets for their products. Some of the country forges and smithies, like those at Mailzie (NX 371541) and

Water wheel formerly at Park Lime works c 1900

Shotts (NX 909912), relied on water as a prime-mover, although the region's best-known smithy, that at Gretna Green (NY 321684), is noted chiefly for the forging of marriages. More in keeping with mechanical traditions was Kirkpatrick McMillan's invention, at Courthill Smithy (NX 856935), of the first pedal-assisted bicycle in about 1840.

The smithy at Shotts was one of several users of the Garroch water-power system. Introduced between 1790 and 1810 primarily as a means of hauling waggons out of the quarries and underground workings of the Park Limeworks (NX 907913), this ingenious water-course ran across a watershed in contoured races, achieving a steady flow over a distance of more than 5 km. It was supplemented at Heathery Dam (NX 9293) by a similarly graded and controlled channel out of Loch Ettrick (NX 9493). The limeworks haulage system had a huge overshot wheel, some 9 m in diameter; the smithy, by contrast, was powered by a diminutive undershot wheel. This water-supply also drove a sawmill and a turbine-operated joiner's shop, recently destroyed by fire. From the limeworks the water flowed underground to the Lake Burn and emptied into the Nith close to Barburgh Mill. The power requirements of this early 19th-century woollen mill may also have formed part of the original scheme.

Former mill building, Ann Street, Gatehouse of Fleet

Houses, Fleet Street, Gatehouse of Fleet

**Tongland Power
Station**

A water-power system of similar ingenuity and extent was devised in about 1790 to serve an ambitious cotton-spinning enterprise at Gatehouse of Fleet (no. 8). At a cost of about £1,400, water for no less than four cotton mills, two tanneries, a brass foundry and a brewery was drawn principally from the west end of Loch Whinyeon (NX 619608) through a tunnel and canalised burn. It was led to a pair of mill dams (NX 603566) from which lades ran down each side of the village serving different sets of mills. The extensive remains of this system cover a distance of over 4.6 km.

Water is still used as a means of generating its modern power successor, electricity. Following old principles but on a much bigger and more sophisticated scale, the Galloway Hydro-Electric Scheme employs a series of seven dams and linked water-courses, even crossing a watershed by means of a 1.7 km-long tunnel from Loch Doon. This public utility was built between 1931 and 1935, and at the time of its completion was the largest integrated installation of its kind in the United Kingdom, incorporating many big and novel engineering features. Fifty years on, its reinforced concrete dams, its surge towers and its five power stations are accepted elements in the Dee and Ken valleys, and all eleven original turbo-generators are still in use, tributes equally to contemporary ideas of environmental and technical design. In summer months, the principal control station at Tongland (NX 695536) is open to visitors by appointment.

The waters of the River Dee have had a more long-standing importance. 'Abundantly plenished with excellent salmon' is how the river was described in 1684, and in the same account we learn that towards the mouth of the river 'Thomas Lidderdail of Isle [St Mary's Isle] hath a large fishyard wherein he gets abundance of salmon and any other fish'. Salmon fishing on a commercial scale has for centuries been an important aspect of Solway life, wicker salmon-traps having been immortalised in the ancient rhyme about the Kennedy family which refers to the 'Cruives of Cree'. Fish farming also has ancient origins. The long narrow channels close to New Abbey Pow to the west of New Abbey village were almost certainly medieval fishponds (NX 962663) stocked to serve the nearby abbey (no. 71). In about 1868 the Solway Fishery at Kinharvie (NX 941661) revived the tradition of pisciculture on the banks of the same waters, and was the first British establishment of its kind to carry out a successful international import-export trade in sporting fish. More remarkable and possibly unique in Scotland is the extraordinary tidal fish pond on the Rhins coast at Port Logan (NX 096413). Here, laboriously blasted out of the natural rock by Colonel Andrew McDouall of Logan between 1788 and 1800, is a basin, 15.2 m in diameter and 9.1 m deep; it is linked to the sea by a narrow cleft which has been blocked sufficiently to allow movement of tidal waters but not of fish. Purposely designed to be stocked with sea fish as a readily available food supply, the pond has become home for generations of tame, trusting and well-fed cod fish.

Over the centuries the quarrying of stone for building purposes has taken place throughout the region, often for specific local needs. But the grey granites of the Stewartry and the splendid red sandstones of Lower Nithsdale and Annandale were building materials of the highest quality and trading potential, once a means of large-scale extraction and finishing became established in the second quarter of the 19th century. The two main original centres of granite quarrying were near where they actively remain (and *not* to be visited), namely, at Kirkmabreck (NX 485567) and Craignair (NX 8160), both sites being well placed to take advantage of water-borne transport. Stewartry granite is much in evidence in engineering works throughout the world, but the shiny little towns of Dalbeattie and Creetown are themselves probably the best, and certainly the most homely monuments to this material. The region's warm and durable sandstones of Permian (New Red Sandstone) and Carboniferous ages can also be seen to best effect in those districts from which they were hewn, particularly in the towns of Dumfries and Annan. These quarries enjoyed a boom period around 1895-1910, when Dumfriesshire sandstone was put to very extensive national and international use. Nowadays, the large sandstone quarry at Locharbriggs (NX 987813) remains the sole working memorial to a once-hectic past.

The region's economic geology provided opportunities for a full range of extractive industries, but none pursued on a significantly large or intensive scale by national standards. A scatter of short-lived metal mines, situated mainly on the fringes of the main granite hill masses, produced workable quantities of lead, copper, iron and, uniquely in Britain, antimony, which was obtained from a mine in Glendinning, Eskdale (NY 298970). But in the annals of metal mining, the village of Wanlockhead (no. 9) occupies a very special place. Together with Leadhills, it has been at the centre of the Scottish lead and precious metal mining industry from the Middle Ages down to the 20th century. The village is the highest in Scotland, and it requires little imagination to appreciate the harsh and lonely circumstances in which the lead-mining community found itself; but the harshness is offset by the magical knowledge that gold and silver really has been found in these hills.

**Corn Mill,
New Abbey**

7* New Abbey, Corn Mill

18th and 19th centuries AD.

*NX 962662. On W side of A 710 near centre of
village; signposted.*

Historic Scotland.

This range of buildings has been described as 'a
classic example of the Galloway country mill'.
Indeed, it may be regarded as representative of the
numberless water-powered grain mills that have
done service throughout Scotland since about 1750,
although every mill, like every miller and almost
every owner, had its own particular way of getting
the work done.

A mill probably stood on or near this site in the
Middle Ages serving the nearby Cistercian
monastery (no. 71), hence the name 'Monksmill' by
which it is still known. The existing building,
however, dates only from the late 18th century, and
was erected by the Stewart family of Shambellie
(no. 22), heirs to part of the medieval monastic
estate. It was altered and heightened to three
storeys during the 19th century, and continued in
commercial use until the Second World War.
Afterwards maintained as a precious relic by Mr
Charles Stewart of Shambellie, it has been restored
with painstaking care by Historic Scotland. The
present condition of the building and its intricate
mechanism reflects great credit on the prescient
efforts of both these parties.

The restored water-wheel, which is affixed to the
rear side-wall, is of a high breastshot or pitchback
type, that is, the water drops on to its wooden
buckets at a point just short of the wheel's vertical
centre line, causing it to turn against the natural
flow. The volume of water striking the wheel, and
hence its speed, can be regulated by a trap-door in
the wooden trough which carries the water to the
wheel.

Inside, following usual Scottish practice, the mill is
'underdrift', that is, the pairs of grinding stones (in
this case, three) are on an upper floor and driven
from below; windmills for instance, are usually
'overdrift' because the power comes from above.
The drive-mechanisms in this mill are thus on the
ground floor directly behind the water-wheel; they
are contained within the timber-framed cupboard
which confronts the visitor on entering the mill.
The main purpose of the gearing is to transmit and
convert the power from the slow-speed, large-
radius and vertically-set turning motion of the
water-wheel outside into a series of high-speed,
small-radius and horizontally rotating millstones
within. It does this through a system of shafts and
gear wheels of different sizes and mesh, some
bevelled, some straight-edged, and one with
wooden teeth. The small gears (the stone nuts) on
the final drive to the stones can be raised and
disengaged when not required.

On the first floor, the three pairs of millstones are
cased in wooden vats, so only the top of the upper
stone of each pair (the mobile or runner stone) can
be seen; the lower stone (the bedstone) remains
static. One set of emery-faced composition stones
operated independently to produce animal
provender. The other sets of stones were used in
succession to obtain oatmeal: the shelling stones
separated the husks and the kernels; the finishing
stones ground the shelled grain (groats) into
finished meal of different grades. These operations
required better quality stones like those lying
outside the mill, which have sandstone centres and
banded segments of quartz. The wooden hoppers
mounted above the stones were fed with dried grain
from the loft above.

The grain was dried in the adjacent kiln, laid on a
perforated iron-tiled floor above a brick-built
furnace. The kiln was fired in a hearth on the

ground floor where a passage-vault, possibly to assist internal ventilation, runs around the outside of the flared furnace-stack. The ventilator cowl on the roof-ridge—a tell-tale indicator of a kiln—is here topped with a weather-vane in the shape of a salmon. Unusually, the kiln and the miller's house have been built as one unit.

These primary processes were supported by a number of ancillary operations: on the ground floor, a winnowing machine and fan (for sieving the husks and blowing them through to the kiln for fuel) and an oats bruiser (for animal feed), no longer extant, were driven from the pit-wheel; on the first floor, a shaking sieve (for refined sifting of meal) was belt-driven from an extended millstone drive-shaft; and in the loft, a pulley-operated sack-hoist was driven from an extension of the main upright shaft.

Finally, and most crucially, water to power the mill was conducted from the northern end of Loch Kindar (NX 964648) on a 1 km-long lade to the pond which lies just to the south-west of the mill. This too has been restored to working order, placid and complete with its sluice-mechanism, its overflow channel—and its ducks!

8 Gatehouse of Fleet, Cotton Mills

18th and 19th centuries AD.

NX 599563, 603563.

With its bright colour-washed buildings, wide streets and hilly tree-clad setting, there could scarcely be a less industrial image than that presented by Gatehouse of Fleet. Yet, for a few decades, this trim little town was the centre of the cotton textile industry in Galloway and stood close to the forefront of the industrial revolution in Scotland. It is this contrast that makes Gatehouse of Fleet such a worthwhile subject for archaeological rediscovery.

In 1785 James Murray of Broughton and Cally, founder of Gatehouse, granted a lease on the banks of the River Fleet in his recently established village to Messrs Birtwhistle and Sons, a Yorkshire firm of cattle-dealers and merchants, who had been thwarted in their initial attempts to build a cotton

mill near Kirkcudbright. They built two water-powered mills; a third mill in the same complex was added by a Mr McWilliam, and a fourth was established at the north-eastern end of the village by the Ulster firm of Thomas Scott and Company. Altogether, these spinning and weaving mills employed a workforce of more than 500, and required the services of a brass foundry to maintain the metal parts of their machinery in running order. By the 1790s the centre of Gatehouse also contained two tanneries, a soapwork (by-products of the cattle trade), and a brewery. As a source of power the Fleet was inadequate, and an elaborate water-course, 6.4 km long, was engineered to draw 'copious streams of water' to two dams at the head of the village. But the river was useful as a means of transport, and to improve access a 1.3 km-long reach between Gatehouse and Skyreburn Bay was canalised in 1824-5. Thanks to David McAdam, a local merchant and shipowner, the shallow landing-place at Boat Green (NX 598560) was replaced in 1836-7 by a new quay at the head of the canal, usable by ships of 300 tons and ever since known as Port McAdam.

By this date, however, the textile industries of Gatehouse had lost their impetus, having been unable to compete with steam-powered and better transport-related mills elsewhere. After Murray's death in 1799 Scott's mill closed, later to be converted into an estate sawmill. The Birtwhistle mills were idle between 1810 and 1832, at which date they were acquired by Messrs James Davidson and Company. Having quickly rebuilt a mill gutted by fire in 1840, this company fought valiantly to remain in business, but survived only until about 1850. Their mills subsequently came into the possession of a firm of timber merchants, who converted one of the buildings into a bobbin mill. Pirns and bobbins were manufactured here until the early 1930s; by that decade the sawmill and barracks that had been Scott's mill had probably become a private house, the main brewery had closed (in 1911), and Port McAdam was being used commercially for the last time.

The best-preserved of the early cotton mills is the three-storeyed building at the head of Ann Street (NX 603563) that began life as Scott's mill. Of the Birtwhistle complex there is a handsomely restored four-storeyed mill (NX 599563) and the overgrown foundations of two others, the positions of the large water-wheels still being discernible. The activities of this firm are also well represented by terraced rows of single- and two-storeyed workers' houses in Birtwhistle Street (NX 601566) and Catherine Street (NX 600565). Other survivors from Gatehouse's industrial heyday include the former brewery (NX 599563), a sizeable three-storeyed and hip-roofed block which stands above the Fleet Bridge; on the opposite side of the High Street, below the Angel Hotel, is the building which used to be the main tannery (NX 599562). The remains of the water-power system are worthy of exploration, and the straight line of the Fleet Canal still presents itself very obviously to view. The remains of the drystone, timber-fronted quay at Port McAdam were repaired in 1975 for use by pleasure craft, one facet of Gatehouse's best-ever industry—tourism and leisure.

9* Wanlockhead, Lead Mines

18th and 19th centuries AD.

NS 8712, 8713, 8613. On the B 797 signposted from the A 76; the village also lies on the Southern Upland Way.

These hills have been mined from time immemorial, possibly since Roman times, and on a commercial basis since 1680. Most of the visible remains, however, are the products of mining and smelting activity during the past two centuries.

They are now cared for by a local museum trust with help from Historic Scotland and Buccleuch Estates Ltd.

From the museum (the old smithy), a visitors' trail runs through the major features of the village. The museum is located on the valley floor close to the Wanlock Water, which flows north-westwards, eventually to empty into a tributary of the River Clyde. It is down this valley that the visitor should proceed, following the track of an old narrow-gauge railway and re-crossing the burn to approach the entrance to Loch Nell Mine.

This mine was first opened in 1710, abandoned, then re-opened and used in its present form from 1793 to the middle of the 19th century. It continued in use as an exit from adjacent mines, and is now open to visitors over a distance of about 200 m. In the second phase it was associated with a deep shaft, still terrifyingly visible within; this in turn was connected with a drainage level under Straitsteps Mine, the next objective on the visitors' trail.

The water-bucket pumping engine above Straitsteps Mine at NS 870131 is the monumental showpiece of Wanlockhead. As befits the only known water-powered beam-engine of its kind in Britain to survive virtually intact, it is a monument in State custody. Its task was to pump water out of abandoned workings, and it performed this function probably from the late 1870s to the early

Wanlockhead village, c 1910

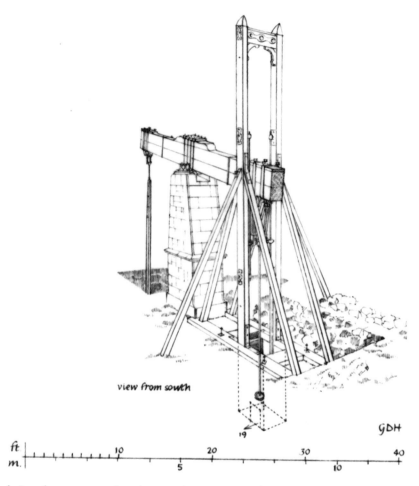

view from south

ᎶᎠᎻ

19

ft 10 20 30 40
m. 5 10

Water-bucket
pumping engine,
Wanlockhead:
perspective
drawing by
GD Hay

1900s. Its design, however, was based on engines used extensively in mining industries well over a century earlier.

To operate the pump, water from a cistern was piped under the road and into a box-like bucket at the end of the beam that is held within the wooden steeple frame. The weight of water depressed that end of the beam, raising the pumping apparatus affixed to the other end. At the bottom of each stroke (about every 30 seconds) the water was released automatically through a valve into a stone-lined drainage pit, causing the pump spear to be lowered, ready to lift its next column of water up the shaft to the drainage level. Affectionately known as 'Bobbing Johns', such devices were relatively simple, and could be left to operate with the minimum of attention. Would that some water in a bucket, or a coin in the slot, could set it all in motion again!

Near the pump there is the circular track of a horse-engine which was at one time used for winding ore and spoil out of the mine. From here, the trail traverses the valley to a modern plinth, which bears a reproduction of a 1775 drawing showing the mining scene from about this viewpoint. The trail then re- crosses the valley to the ruins of Pates Knowe Smelt Mill. When it was built in 1764 this mill was only one of a number on the Wanlock Water, but in about 1789 it was enlarged in order to smelt all the mined ore. In 1845 it was partly dismantled in order to build a new mill downstream. Excavation has revealed the outline of two 'back-to-back' furnace houses sharing a central water-driven bellows house. The cast-iron 'Scotch ore' smelting hearths are rare survivors from the 18th century, and the ore and slag hearths in the eastern half of the building have been partly restored to give an impression of their original appearance.

Lead mines, Wanlockhead, c 1775

Equally significant discoveries have been made at the Bay Mine (NS 868137), the furthest point on the industrial trail. The visible remains represent successive attempts to pump water out of this area of particularly deep mines. Stone mountings are all that survive of the atmospheric steam pumping engine which operated here from 1790 to 1799. Upon the re-opening and deepening of the mine (to 152.4 m) after 1842, a hydraulic pump was introduced alongside a steam-powered winding engine, but even these combined arrangements could not cope with the flooding effects of torrential rains. In the 1880s an auxiliary pump was built purposely to be driven by floodwater. The surviving stone-built pit shows that it must have had a big 9.1 m diameter wheel, no doubt a memorable sight as it turned in the pouring rain.

There is, of course a human, as well as an industrial side to the Wanlockhead story, which is best told by the buildings in the village, by the monuments in the burial ground (NS 864136), and by the museum exhibits. The whole village is known to have been rebuilt by the Quaker Company in the decade after their lease of 1710. Again, after 1842, when the Dukes of Queensberry took a direct stake in the running of the mines and in the welfare of the workforce, the houses were rebuilt and their numbers increased. When direct ducal control ended in 1906 there were about 173 inhabited dwellings in the village and Meadowfoot. Many had upper storeys, slated roofs and dressed stonework, but, a substantial proportion had

steeply-pitched, heather-thatched roofs concealing boxed 'lums'. The ruins of one such terraced row can be seen by the roadside on the return journey from Bay Mine.

The community buildings were also built or rebuilt in the middle decades of the 19th century. As an institution, however, Wanlockhead Library is second only to Leadhills as the oldest subscription library in Britain. In 1756, 32 men of the village, mostly miners, subscribed to a reading society 'for the purpose of purchasing books for our mutual improvement'. The first purpose-built library was erected in 1788, and the present building was put up in 1850 to accommodate a much-expanded collection. It was last used as a lending library in the 1930s.

Main-line railways arrived in the neighbouring valleys in the mid 19th century, and a branch-line railway ran between Wanlockhead and Elvanfoot from 1902 to 1938. In the early days most lead was carted to Leith, and if the visitor follows this route on his return journey he will see the surviving evidence of rival concerns in the neighbouring village of Leadhills (NS 8814; Clydesdale District, Strathclyde Region). The mining grounds here were owned by the Hope family from the 1640s, and contributed to Hopetoun House, their grand mansion in West Lothian. The mines were closed in 1928, and, compared to Wanlockhead, the centre of Leadhills now exhibits considerably less of its industrial origins.

3
TOWNS AND VILLAGES

Dumfries
High Street
and Mid Steeple:
19th-century
engraving

As economists point out, industry, services and communications are essential to the success of any modern town; these elements are its heart, its lifeblood and its arteries. It has always been thus, and the vicissitudes of trade and industry provide a background against which the historic towns of the region can be seen and understood. But just as Dumfries and Galloway escaped the grosser effects of industrialisation, neither has the area been heavily urbanised. Towns are not scarce, but they are evenly spaced out and most still retain the intimate size and character of small country market-centres.

Even Dumfries would be well down the urban league table of central Scotland. It has always been the dominant regional capital, and in recent centuries many forms of industry and commerce came together in Dumfries, giving it a strongly Georgian and Victorian architectural character (no. 11). The physical tone of modern Dumfries was set, never to be surpassed, by the municipality's own Mid Steeple (no. 10). Built with the fruits of a financial windfall, this stylish three-storeyed town house symbolised the town's proud estimation of its own civic status and commercial prowess at a time when Dumfries ranked sixth among the royal burghs of Scotland. Just as the Mid Steeple stands for modern Dumfries, so the old bridge (no. 4) symbolises the medieval town; standing at the upper tidal limit and lowest bridging-point of the River Nith, this was the gateway to Galloway. William I formally established the king's burgh of Dumfries in 1186, the first chartered burgh in this region and the only one that continuously maintained its royal status. To the south-east, Dumfries was partly protected by the Lochar Moss, a considerable expanse of marshland which probably saved the burgh from the worst effects of the long-drawn-out wars with England. The town, it may be added, has long attracted favourable comment from visitors, and Tobias Smollett's opinion, expressed through one of the characters in *The Expedition of Humphry Clinker* (1771) is typical. To him, Dumfries was 'a very elegant trading town ... where we found plenty of good provision and excellent wine, at very reasonable prices, and the accommodation as good in all respects as in any part of South Britain. If I was confined to Scotland for life, I would choose Dumfries as the place of my residence'.

Annan Bridge: sketch drawing, 1902

Like Dumfries, the Bruce-founded burgh of Annan (NY 1966) grew up by the side of a defended river-crossing, but it stood close to a main route from the south and was a front-line target in times of Anglo-Scottish conflict. From its first destruction by the English in 1298 until after 1660, Annan had little respite from warring armies to take full advantage of its chartered privileges. However, it was the erosive waters of the River Annan which, in about 1200, brought about the first of Annan's calamities. Allegedly manifesting a curse laid upon the lords of Annandale by St Malachy, the river evidently washed away part of the castle, forcing the Bruces to make their principal residence at Lochmaben, and causing Annan a temporary loss of its burghal dignity. In the middle of the 15th century the Annandale estates passed from the Douglases to the Crown, and by 1532 Annan had become a royal burgh, a status which conferred many constitutional and commercial benefits, including a local monopoly of external trade.

The castle (NY 191667; private garden) still bears the scars of river erosion, but, except in its position and layout, the town betrays little physical trace of its ancient and turbulent past. The earliest standing buildings are of 18th-century date, the modern town being the product of two centuries of undisturbed agricultural industries and trade. To the visitor, the memorable qualities of this one-time frontier town are visual and tangible, not historical: its riverside setting, its deep red sandstone, and its solid Victorian architecture, epitomised by a large town hall rebuilt in 1877.

Lochmaben (NY 0882), too, shows few built signs of its early origins, although its wide and spacious High Street with medial expansion for a market-place does preserve part of a medieval layout of linear form. A small but elegant town hall (1723 and 1878) with its steeple (1743) stands at the head of the High Street, and the restored market cross has been re-positioned nearby. The oldest houses date from the middle decades of the 18th century. By-passed by modern trunk routes, the town has the atmosphere of a quiet pre-industrial community, but with its two attendant castles (no. 42) stands on what was once the main road into upper Nithsdale. As a

Lochmaben:
aerial view

Bruce-founded burgh which passed to the Douglases and then to the Crown, Lochmaben's medieval history parallels that of Annan except in its documentation; the first record of burghal status was not until 1296, but royal superiority was recorded almost immediately after the Douglas forfeiture in 1440.

Wigtown (NX 4355) conveys even more the impression of a community that has been in gentle retirement for a few centuries. It was never in the forefront of military conflict, but in the 16th and 17th centuries witnessed fierce battles of a political kind which this latter-day calm belies. These battles were fought in defence of the royal burgh's trading freedoms' (meaning its monopoly) throughout western Galloway against the promotions of Whithorn (1511) and Stranraer (1617) to the same status.

Like Dumfries, Wigtown grew up alongside a royal castle and sheriffdom, and was a royal burgh by 1292, possibly even before 1263. It was in the possession of the Fleming family from 1341 to 1372 and then of the Douglases until their forfeiture in 1455, when the burgh returned to a position of direct dependence on the king. However, the physical character and even the position of early Wigtown remain something of a mystery. According to Symson in 1684, the town 'as the inhabitants say, of old stood more than a mile eastward, but [this] place is now covered with the sea every tide'. On its later hillside site Wigtown may have lost, or be secretly concealing, houses built for the local gentry. In 1549, for example, royal permission was granted to a kinsman of the Hannays of Sorbie to heighten and project the upperworks of his town house and to give it corbelled battlements. In 1684 we know that the town had 'pretty good houses three stories high toward the street, especially on the north side', a storey higher than the average provincial town at that date.

For a more complete picture of a small provincial town the visitor should turn to Kirkcudbright (nos 12-14), the county town of the Stewartry and the outstanding historic town of the region. To walk the streets of old Kirkcudbright is to experience a gentle ambience that is without parallel in urban Scotland, a special quality which

Old mercat cross and houses, Wigtown

has attracted generations of artists and writers. Dorothy L Sayers, one of the doyennes of crime fiction, captured this mood in inter-war Kirkcudbright in her novel, *Five Red Herrings* (1931), whilst Sir Walter Scott used the tolbooth (no. 12) as a model for the prison which plays a grim character part in Chapter 23 of *Guy Mannering* (1815).

As with Wigtown, however, today's benign calm belies the turmoil of a past in which the town found itself on the defensive, militarily, as it warded off English-inspired invasions in the 16th century and, commercially, as it tried to maintain its monopoly against 'unfree' trade within its 'liberties'. Although there is no record of its status as a burgh until 1330, there was almost certainly an urban community here in the later 13th century. It must have been included in the grant to Archibald Douglas in 1369, and upon that family's forfeiture in 1455 a royal charter made Kirkcudbright again a 'free [i.e. royal] burgh'.

The urban architecture of Kirkcudbright goes back to the last quarter of the 16th century (no. 13), but its historic value extends beyond the intrinsic merits of its excellent town houses. It is now the only place in the region where the relationship of the early town, river, and castle (no. 40) can be easily appreciated. Indeed, the river has had a considerable influence on the layout of the town. The car park at Harbour Square is an infilled boat-dock, constructed between about 1817 and 1825 across what used to be a tidal river creek. This creek and its associated marshlands had extended quite far south and east, partly encircling the High Street on its raised gravel ridge. Given the high tidal rise of the Dee, Kirkcudbright would have had a strikingly insular aspect, and even as late as 1844 Lord Cockburn was able to describe the town as 'the Venice of Scotland'.

Old Clachan in the Glenkens was one of the 'illegal' market centres that were a source of irritation to Kirkcudbright; it fiercely opposed the proposal to erect St John's Clachan of Dalry (NX 6281) into a royal burgh in 1629. The scheme ran into difficulties of its own, largely through lack of co-operation on the part of the local laird, and was transferred to lands further south which had a better disposed owner. But the auguries for New Galloway (NX 6377) were not good; Lord Kenmure, the owner, died shortly after the burgh's foundation, it was not as well placed for trade as 'Old Galloway' (Old Clachan), and has remained the smallest burgh in Scotland with a population of less than 350.

Kirkcudbright, by William Daniell, 1814

New Galloway, the last and the smallest of the region's nine royal burghs, was surpassed by a number of burghs of barony and regality whose constitutional and commercial privileges were of a more restricted order. Some had natural vigour as centres for markets and fairs, in which the cattle trade undoubtedly played a part. Gatehouse of Fleet, for example, had an autumn 'market for good fat kine' more than a century before it became a burgh.

Although urban growth might be casual and adventitious, a degree of planning can be detected in the regularity of street layouts and property boundaries. However, the era of modern planning in relation to building design only began to dawn during the course of the 17th century. A feu-contract of 1628 relating to houses in Langholm provides a precocious example of such planning, possibly the earliest known instance in the country, Unfortunately, the buildings themselves no longer survive, but the region boasts a fine series of planned villages, few more successful than the first, Newton Stewart (NX 4165). Formed out of the riverside village of Fordhouse of Cree, it was founded as a burgh of barony in 1677 by William Stewart of nearby Castle Stewart. The burgh quickly found a niche for itself in the local economy, and to a minister writing in 1793 its growth had simply been amazing'. Its then owner, William Douglas, an enterprising landowner and entrepreneur, was unable to effect a permanent change in the name of the town (to Newton Douglas) and in its industrial base. At Castle Douglas (NX 7662) in 1791 he had greater success when he erected the village of Carlingwark into an eponymous burgh of barony. Physically, the regular gridded street-plan of Castle Douglas remains close to the planning ideals of the late 18th century, spacious enough to cope with Victorian grandeur and even modern traffic. Newton Stewart, on the other hand, found less sympathy with later commentators. One complained that builders had raised 'their houses high or low, small or great, on a line with others or in recesses or projections, as caprice, accident or convenience suggested. Irregularity has been so far corrected that the place now consists chiefly of a long principal street, with the town-house in the centre'.

But planned urban ideals did not end for ever in the first half of the 19th century. The early 20th-century housing estates at Gretna (NY 3167) and Eastriggs (NY 2566) are now gaining the wider acclaim that is their due. They were built for the Ministry of Munitions between 1915 and 1917 to accommodate workers at an explosives factory, and, in contrast to similar projects elsewhere, their seminal importance lay in the symmetrically ordered arrangement of the houses and their simple neo-Georgian designs. These features were adopted for public housing built in accordance with the Housing and Town Planning Act of 1919, so most English (but paradoxically not Scottish) council houses of the inter-war period will find their roots at Gretna.

Planned and semi-planned villages of 18th- and 19th-century date have become an accepted and 'traditional' feature of the region's landscape, and few ancient rural communities were left comparatively unaffected by these trends. One such special group of villages is that known as the Royal Four Towns of Lochmaben: Hightae (NY 0978), Smallholm (NY 0977), Greenhill (NY 1079) and Heck (NY 0980), which are associated with fertile holms on the western bank of the River Annan. Their buildings are unremarkable, although there are more 18th-century date-stones than one normally finds in Scottish villages. They are remarkable in the matter of legal tenure which has conditioned a resilient building and settlement pattern. The 'kindly tenants' or rentallers here, who hold immediately of the Crown, are the only survivors of a once-numerous class of medieval tenantry, the closest analogy on the Scottish mainland to English freeholders. These tenancies may have originated as rewards granted out of the castle lands of Lochmaben (no. 42) to the loyal followers of Robert Bruce, and this belief afforded the tenants the special protection of successive kings and parliaments against local officials and lairds.

However, many ancient communities suffered the effects of desertion and decay. About ten of the region's early burgh foundations may never have been more than 'parchment burghs', but some such as Innermessan (NX 0863) and perhaps Urr (no. 44) may well have had genuine urban existences before their functions and privileges lapsed. Villages such as Ruthwell and Amisfield 'Town' probably stand close to earlier burghs bearing those names, whilst the sites of other decayed burghs in Nithsdale such as Terregles (Terreglestown, NX 9476) and Dalgarnock (mid-way between Thornhill and Closeburn) are reasonably well known. The position of the burgh of Preston (1663), which flourished sufficiently to incur Kirkcudbright's wrath, is now marked by a mercat cross (NX 969564), one of the few surviving monuments of this class in the region.

Former town house, Victoria Street, Newton Stewart

Preston mercat cross (Far right)

10 Dumfries, Mid Steeple

AD 1707.

NX 972761. In the centre of the High Street.

In April, 1703, having received a sum of 20,000 merks from the sale of their share of the Tack of Customs and Foreign Excise, the magistrates of Dumfries resolved to spend the money in the building of a new town house. They felt that 'the town is not at present provided with sufficient prisons, whereby several malefactors guilty of great crimes, and others for debt, have made their escape, to the dishonour and imminent peril of the burgh; ... also that there is not a steeple in the whole town, nor a suitable council house and clerk's chamber for keeping the charter chest and records of the burgh, nor a magazine house, nor room for the sure keeping of the town's arms and ammunition ...'.

The Steeple Committee engaged a Liverpool architect John Moffat, to 'furnish a model'. His design was based on the College steeple in Glasgow, and in early 1705 the committee turned to Tobias Bachop of Alloa, one of Sir William Bruce's trusted mason-architects, to put it into effect. Timber was obtained from Garlies Wood above Newton Stewart, and Bachop agreed to supply other building materials. He was to construct the

building 'conform to the scheme drawn, and the alterations of the dimensions which the Committee had made' by Martinmas (11 November) 1707—which he did. The balustrade of the external forestair was completed in scrolled wrought iron, not stone as originally intended, and was the work of an Edinburgh smith, Patrick Sibbald. The total cost was just less than £1,700, out of which Bachop's contract had been for the equivalent of about £1,050.

The masonry, partly refaced, is of red sandstone ashlar throughout, channelled on the lowest storey and on the quoins. Each level is marked by a moulded string-course, and the uppermost levels have pierced stone parapets, the steeple being topped with a lead-covered wooden flèche. The main doorway is at first-floor level in the south end wall, reached by the external forestair. The principal meeting rooms and offices were originally on the first floor of the council chamber block sandwiched between a ground-floor guard house and tron (weights office) and a series of second-floor prison-cells.

There are two relief carved panels on the south wall: the upper one bears a royal armorial, the lower one the figure of St Michael, below which there is the iron mileage panel of 1827 (see Chapter 2). In the west wall there are two inscribed stones from the building's late 16th-century predecessor. It was demolished in 1719, but at the end of the 18th century an old prison block still stood 'nearly adjoining' the town house.

Dumfries,
Mid Steeple (Left)

11 Dumfries, Houses and Hostelries

18th and 19th centuries AD.

NX 9776.

The earliest standing domestic building is Bridge End House on the western approach to the old bridge (no. 4); it dates from about 1662 when Bridgend was a separate suburb. Within Dumfries itself there are some 18th-century houses of formal appearance in Irish Street (eg no. 75) and at 24 Nith Place (*c* 1753). Plainer two- and three-storeyed frontages are to be found in English Street, nos 47-53 perhaps being as early as the mid 18th century. A two-storeyed building in nearby

Loreburn Street was cruck-framed, one of few urban examples found in Scotland; the building has gone, but the crucks are in store at the Nithsdale District Museum. Historical and literary associations are more powerful preservatives, and at 24 Burns Street (originally Millbrae) a plain but homely two-storeyed house of c 1745 date is where Robert Burns lived from 1793 until his death in 1796. Late Georgian or Regency housing is well represented by the terraces in Castle Street and George Street, while the Theatre Royal in Shakespeare Street/Queen Street is the only surviving theatre of the Georgian period in Scotland. It was opened in 1792, enlarged and altered in 1830 and 1876, and served as a cinema from 1911 to 1954; it was re-opened as a theatre in 1960.

Kirkcudbright Tolbooth (Right)

Globe Close, Dumfries: 19th-century engraving

Facing the ornamental fountain (1882, on an older fountain site) at the south end of the High Street are the former Commercial (latterly County) and King's Arms Hotels with their restored frontages. The King's Arms was associated with Burns, as was the Globe Inn, which has a congested but convivial setting down a close at 56 High Street; beneath the whitewash it appears to be of 18th-century or earlier brickwork. The Hole in the Wall' occupies a

similar position closer to the northern end of the High Street (no. 156), and possibly dates from 1620.

12 Kirkcudbright, Tolbooth

AD 1625-7.

NX 680508. At the right-angled corner of the High Street.

This large church-like building stands at the corner of the High Street in Kirkcudbright, a striking terminal feature of the vista from each direction. Together with the group of 17th- and 18th-century houses to the east, it symbolises Kirkcudbright in a manner which no other building manages to achieve. The tower and spire contribute to its visual qualities, but it is by no means the most refined, the biggest, nor even the oldest building in the town. What the tolbooth possesses in strong measure is quite simply character.

The building betrays much evidence of additions and alterations. The western third was added, as was the eastern end, accompanied by the forestair.

The tower itself is of a distinctly different masonry and style, and represents a third addition. There are now only vestiges of the main doorway with its round-headed moulded surround. Large windows lit the main rooms on the first floor, and small ones were associated with prison-cells on the upper floor.

On the landing of the forestair is the mercat cross of 1610. It was moved here in the 19th century from a position now marked by a flat sunken stone in the High Street north of the tolbooth. The base of the forestair contains a well, and a plaque commemorates the introduction of gravitation water-supply in 1762-3. Other details include the old iron 'jougs', by which malefactors were publicly manacled, and on top of the spire a weather-vane in the form of a sailing-ship, said to commemorate the Battle of Trafalgar in 1805. The clock is modern, but its square-dialled, one-handed predecessor is still preserved in the Stewartry Museum. Possibly of Dutch origin, it was in existence by 1576 and was installed in this building in about 1642. There is a bell of 1646, and one of 1724 which is now in the museum.

The nucleus of this building was erected during a two-year period after 30 March 1625. At that date the provost and magistrates of the burgh obtained a grant (taken out of the fines of the commission of the justices of the peace) towards building a tolbooth and strong prison-house 'within the heart and body of their town'. A subvention towards works of repair was recorded in 1731. It was eventually replaced as town hall by the building erected in 1878 at the junction of St Mary's Street and Church Street.

Literary fame arrived earlier, for the tolbooth was almost certainly the model for the prison in the denouement of Scott's *Guy Mannering*.

Kirkcudbright Tolbooth: spire and weather-vane
(Left)

Clock and mechanism in Stewartry Museum
(Bottom left)

13 MacLellan's Castle, Kirkcudbright

c AD 1582.

NX 682510. At the junction of Castle Street and St Cuthbert Street; signposted.

Historic Scotland.

The sight of this substantial tower-house near the centre of Kirkcudbright often elicits surprise, mainly because it makes absolutely no concessions to the demands of an urban environment. But it is this very quality that provides the key to our understanding of this building and the self-esteem of its builder, Sir Thomas MacLellan of Bombie. At the time of the house's completion in about 1582,

Thomas was provost of Kirkcudbright, held much property in the town and county, and was shortly to marry, as his second wife, Dame Grissel Maxwell, daughter of the powerful Lord Herries. This house is nothing less than the mark of a wealthy and ambitious burgess-laird, and his monument (1597) inside the nearby Greyfriars Church is of an equally grand and elaborate style. His son, Robert, became 1st Lord Kirkcudbright in 1633, but the family's enthusiasm for the Royalist cause and military adventures, particularly in

Ireland, were to cost them dear. During the minority of 4th Lord Kirkcudbright between 1664 and 1669 the estates were seized by the family's creditors, and there was virtually nothing left to support the title.

The rise and fall of the House of MacLellan is reflected in the house itself, which may not have seen further use beyond the end of the 17th century. Indeed, there are traditions that some of the upper-floor rooms had always been in an unfinished state, but in any case by 1752 the roof and internal fittings were stripped out. Despite its gun-ports, angle-turrets, and a forbidding general mien, this building was essentially a domestic, not a defensive, security-conscious pile. Large windows, plenty of stairs (including a straight-flighted main stair), dry closets in place of open latrines, more than fifteen heated rooms, a well laid-out service basement with a kitchen in the wing and vaulted stores in the main block—these are the points that a late 16th-century estate agent would have spotted immediately. But, for all its complex novelty and sophistication, the design follows traditional medieval lines in being centred around a first-floor hall with its adjacent chamber.

MacLellan's Castle, Kirkcudbright

MacLellan's Castle, Kirkcudbright: conjectural reconstruction of hall

This room - the family dining room - as it may have looked in its heyday in the 1590s.

It is worth emphasising two of the more significant details. Above the door in the re-entrant angle there is a framed and pedimented set of three panels which contain relief carvings of what was probably the royal arms above those of Sir Thomas MacLellan and of Lord Herries, the latter bearing the initials G(rissel) M(axwell) and the date 1582. Within the great hall, and commensurate with the scale of the whole establishment, is an imposing fireplace which Sir Thomas's banqueting guests could not have failed to notice. He could have noticed them, too, even if he was not present, for cut into the back of the fireplace is a neat spy-hole or 'laird's lug', through which, as one account puts it, 'observation could be maintained on the occupants of the hall'.

14* Broughton House, High Street, Kirkcudbright

Mid 18th century AD.

NX 681510. On the W side of the northern limb of the High Street.

This is the most distinguished house in a street full of pleasant domestic architecture of the Georgian period. It takes its name from Broughton in Wigtownshire (NX 4544), the original seat of the Murray family. The house was erected by James Murray, builder of Cally (no. 23), probably shortly after he succeeded his father in 1750. It received additions in the 19th century, and a long gallery wing was designed for the artist, E A Hornel, in 1909-10.

Unlike most of its neighbours, the house is set back from the street, fronting on to a railed and paved forecourt. Its appearance is an attractive blend of formal and traditional: its symmetrical five-bay elevation is centred around a period doorway but is set within random rubble masonry walls which rise centrally to a pedimented gablet. The blind oculus and cylindrical scrolled skewputs are a typical touch for houses of this date and status.

The house has some good panelled interiors, especially in the hall and the south room. The main focus of attention nowadays, however, is Hornel's work as an artist and Edwardian home creator. The

Broughton House, High Street, Kirkcudbright

garden is equally exotic, laid out in Japanese style but incorporating native Scottish gatepiers, sundials, and an early cross-slab from Dalshangan near Carsphairn.

Stranraer Castle

15 Stranraer Castle

c AD 1500 and early 19th century.

NX 060608. In the town centre near the junction of Castle Street and Charlotte Street.

Long hidden away and scarcely known, even by the town's inhabitants, this four-storeyed tower is once again prominent in the centre of Stranraer. Its re-emergence in this manner is very fitting, for, from its first construction by the Adairs of Kinhilt in about 1500 until the later 18th century, the 'Castle of Chapel' would have dominated the surrounding community of low, mainly single-storeyed buildings. It was in existence almost a century before the formal creation of Stranraer as a burgh of barony in 1595 (a royal burgh in 1617).

The medieval chapel which gave its name to the tower was a dependency of the parish church of Inch, 4.8 km to the east. The late medieval chapel building itself was demolished in the late 17th or early 18th century. The original community of

Stranraer proper, on the other hand, lay within the medieval parish of Leswalt, centred 4.8 km away to the north-west. Stranraer thus represents a coalescence of two settlements which had grown up on a mutual parish boundary; even today most of the town is divided between the parishes of Inch and Leswalt, the line of the burn and the old parish boundary marked physically by the natural hollow between the castle and George Street.

The tower is of conventional late medieval form. Originally it was of three main storeys with a parapet wall-walk and angle-turrets, all open to the skies; the main stair, later diverted at ground-level, is in the projecting wing. The top storey is an addition, and the small round-headed windows (easily distinguished from original lintelled openings) are part of a scheme of modifications carried out in about 1820. At that date the first floor of the tower was converted into a courtroom, three (criminal) cells were formed on the second floor and two (debtors') cells on the third. The building was converted into a police station in 1864, and some prison-cells apparently remained in use until 1907.

Although altered, the building retains much of its original cellular form of construction, the walls containing a network of passages and chambers. The pit-prison was at the rear of the hall fireplace on the first floor reached through a trap-door on the floor above. The 1820 prison-cells still possess many of their awesomely strong and heavy fittings, and on the walls of the cells and parapet there is a lot of graffiti. Such marks speak volumes.

The tower passed into the possession of a branch of the Kennedy family in 1590, and for a time after 1682 became the headquarters of Graham of Claverhouse, for ever remembered as 'Bloody Clavers' in his role as sheriff of Wigtown.

We know that in 1684 Stranraer had merely 279 inhabitants over the age of 12, but by the end of the 18th century it contained 'many handsome houses and above two thousand inhabitants', most dependent on seasonal shoals of herring in Loch Ryan. This capricious fish finally abandoned the loch in the early 19th century, but the sagging fortunes of the town were revived by its assumption of the Irish steam packet and ferry service.

The earliest surviving municipal building is the former town house (now Stranraer Museum) of 1776 at the corner of George Street and Church Street. Although its official duties were done by 1855, it still conveys an impression of civic dignity with its pedimented door-piece rising to a stubby clock tower and spire. According to an 1877 guide 'It is ... like some ladies—not Stranraer ladies, however—very much indebted to paint for its good looks'. Cosmetically treated or not, the faces of many town houses look out over the loch, and its largest Victorian mansion stands close to the harbour. This is the North-West Castle, now a hotel, which was so named and extended by Sir John Ross (1777-1856), famous for his exploration of Canada's Arctic coastline in search of the elusive North West Passage.

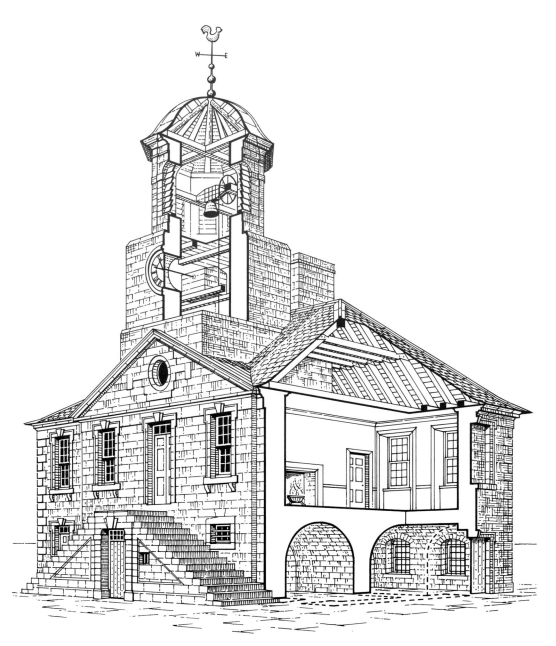

Sanquhar Town House: perspective section by J Borland

16 Sanquhar, Town House

AD 1735.

NS 780099. In the town centre on the W side of the A 76; Sanquhar is on the Southern Upland Way.

Motorists on the A 76 are not in a position to appreciate the finer points of a building which partially restricts their passage through the centre of Sanquhar. But this building has the right of way over modern traffic; it has been here since 1735 and is one of the most handsome early Georgian town houses in the country. It was designed by William Adam, and built at the expense of the 3rd Duke of Queensberry (d. 1778). Materials for its building were partly provided by the ruins of Sanquhar Castle.

It is a two-storeyed block with a square clock tower and octagonal cupola rising above the main five-bay and pedimented frontage. A double-sided forestair leads to a central first-floor entrance. The building is not normally accessible, but the grander meeting- rooms and offices were probably on the first floor, and there may have been ground-floor cells behind the forestair. The northernmost first-floor room is known to have a large 16th-century fireplace taken from the castle.

Although promoted to royal burgh status in 1598, Sanquhar's main period of growth did not come until the early 19th century with the expansion of its staple industry of coal mining, supplemented by the manufacture of worsteds. Sketchy knowledge of its early layout is gained from a document of 1508,

and a census of 1684 showed that the number of adult inhabitants was then precisely 167. The top of the former mercat cross (1680) is built into St Ninian's Free Church, and some buildings in the High Street may be hiding 17th-century origins. The little bow-windowed shop at 39-41 High Street declares itself to be the oldest Post Office in Great Britain (1763).

17 The 'Arched House', Ecclefechan

Late 18th century AD.

NY 193745. In the centre of the village, signposted from the A 74 and the B 725.

NTS.

Ecclefechan ('little church') is the birthplace of the great 19th-century philosopher-historian, Thomas Carlyle (1795-1881), the 'Arched House', where he was born, and the tombstone in the churchyard (NY 192744), where he is interred, being the twin objectives of historical pilgrimage.

By village standards the house is of middling size, a longish two-storeyed block with a central elliptically arched pend (passage). It is divided over the pend into two separate houses with their own doorways. A pair of windows above the arch is linked and framed in such a way as to give the effect of a small Venetian window. Carlyle himself recorded that the house was built by his father and uncle, both masons, to serve as conjoined dwellings, and was completed shortly before his birth, probably in about 1791. There are later additions at the back, and a 1673 date-stone is in re-use above the south doorway. Inside, the house contains Carlyle memorabilia, to which furnishings and artefacts have been added in order to re-create the authentic atmosphere of a village home of about 1800.

Thomas's parents moved to another larger house in the village when he was still in his infancy. The remote farmhouse of Craigenputtock (NX 771823), 20.9 km north-west of Dumfries, was inherited from his wife's family, and was their home from 1828 until they moved to London in 1834. Here he wrote the weird romantic masterpiece, *Sartor Resartus.*

The 'Arched House', Ecclefechan

COUNTRY LIFE

Ellisland Farm

Early glimpses into the life-style of rural and urban tenantry are rare but revealing. On a journey in 1629, for example, an English traveller lodged in one building 'where the fire is in the midst of the house ... At Langholm ... house, the wall of it being one course of stones, another sods of earth; it had a door of wicker rods, and the spider webs hung over our heads'.

Physical evidence for habitations of this period is not easy to detect, although a complex pattern of ancient settlement in the area around the Water of Luce has emerged as a result of aerial and terrestrial survey. Comparable work in Eskdale brought to light a settlement at Boyken Burn (NY 314893-311890) which incorporated the remains of at least 29 platform-buildings. So far, few sites have been tested by archaeological excavation. Such investigations at Kirkconnel (NY 250755) failed to produce conclusive structural evidence of a suspected medieval village, while those at the upland township of Polmaddy (no. 19) in the Glenkens were restricted to one season's work. However, Polmaddy still gives a good impression of a small rural community of a bygone age, perhaps typical of many in the Galloway uplands that were abandoned in the 18th and early 19th centuries.

The buildings at Polmaddy are reduced to their foundations, but detailed word-pictures enable us to visualise buildings of similar status and date elsewhere in the region. Writing of the first Wigtownshire farmhouse that he served in, probably towards the end of the 18th century and probably in the vicinity of Kirkinner (NX 4251), Samuel Robinson in his *Reminiscences of Wigtownshire* recalled that 'it stood or rather leant against a piece of rising ground from which the surface was dug away, and the floor underwent no further preparation, so that the one end of the erection stood perhaps 6 feet [1.83 m] higher than the other—that is to say, they built on the incline as they found it'. He went on to describe how the cruck frames were erected, 'four in number on a house of 50 feet [15.24 m] in length', and then thatched. 'The stones were gathered promiscuously, a little mortar of lime, or oftener soil, and the mason proceeded by building two thick gables, with a flue in one of them, and filling up the spaces between the uprights ... No plasterer or joiner was needed in what is called finishing, but a huge lum of bramble and straw was stuck up to do duty in the kitchen end, and a small chimney in the other—the ridge having the same incline as the floor. But rough and uncouth as the structure seemed, when the floor was swept up and a bright fire blazing on the ground, there was a show of rude homely comfort about it ... Immediately in front, at right angles to the house, at a sufficient distance to allow a carriage to pass, stood a small house called the "chammer", a kind of lumber-room, in which was a bed for the two indoor male servants'. The cottar-house 'might be 25 feet [7.62 m] by 15 [4.57 m], in which space were sheltered the hind and his family, and, in very many cases, the cow and poultry; while the pig had a bedroom outside, but ate his meals in the kitchen, and the poultry dined on the crumbs he left'.

These were the buildings of a 400-acre (160 ha) farm, and the old farmhouse must have been similar to the cottage at Torthorwald (no. 18). Clay construction is another tradition which parts of Wigtownshire share with the eastern half of the region (no. 20), particularly around the Solway Plain. The most vivid description of clay-building practices relates to Dornock (NY 2366) where the last-known building of this kind was demolished in 1965. Here, at the end of the 18th century, 'the farm-houses in general, and all the cottages are built of mud or clay; yet these houses, when plastered and properly finished within (as many of them are) are exceeding warm and comfortable. The manner of erecting them is singular. In the first place, they dig out the foundation of the house, and lay a row or two of stones, then they procure from a pit contiguous, as much clay or brick-earth as is sufficient to form the walls: and having provided a quantity of straw, or other litter to mix with the clay, upon a day appointed, the whole neighbourhood, male and female, to the number of 20 or 30, assemble, each with a dung-fork, a spade, or some such instrument. Some fall to the working the clay or mud, by mixing it with straw; others carry the materials; and 4 or 6 of the most experienced hands, build and take care of the walls. In this manner, the walls of the house are finished in a few hours; after which, they retire to a good dinner and plenty of drink which is provided for them, where they have music and a dance, with which, and other marks of festivity, they conclude the evening. This is called a "daubing"; and in this manner they make a frolic of what would otherwise be a very dirty and disagreeable job'.

In the early days of agricultural improvement the enclosures created by the cattle-owning lairds provoked a strong reaction on the part of the evicted tenantry and their followers. The Levellers Rising of 1724-5 was a widespread popular revolt against these 'stone fences', and was sufficiently effective to remind landowners that tenant welfare was an aspect of countryside management that could not be ignored. Later improvers were more mindful of the mutual benefits of landlord-tenant cooperation, particularly on the better farming lands. As the author of the second agricultural survey of Dumfriesshire (1812) put it: 'Proprietors of land are now sensible that, in order to induce men of capital and respectability to live on their farms, it is necessary to accommodate them with good farmhouses, and convenient offices. Few good farms can be stocked and improved unless the farmer can raise a considerable sum as capital: and men of substance are not willing to live in hovels, when they pay handsome rents ... Most landholders, when they let their farms, allow a sum for buildings proportioned to the rent of the farm'.

Thatched cottages, Knowehead: old photograph

The agricultural landscape shows that these principles were applied to most aspects of farming practice and farmstead design. Steadings were henceforth organised on regular lines, the square or courtyard grouping being the most favoured form. The single- or two-storeyed farmhouse generally occupied the centre of the sunny, south-facing range, flanked by byres and stables on the one side, and by barns, granaries and cart-sheds on the other. At the eastern end of a range of offices, the dwelling was better protected from the swirling blast of prevailing south-westerly winds. Many farmhouses stood detached completely from the steading, usually deriving their symmetrical appearance and plan from earlier lairds' houses, although function continued to govern the relative positions of the different units. In the words of the Dumfriesshire survey, 'the stable ought not to be too remote from the house, nor from the yard where the hay of sown grasses is ...; ... the byre ... ought to be convenient ... for meadow hay ... near the calves, and, if possible, also to the kitchen and the dairy; and ... the piggery should be near the steaming-house ... (or) the kitchen'.

Ellisland Farm (no. 21) is a useful example of a small tenant-holding preserved in a late 18th-century semi-improved state. But elsewhere visitors will see grander dwellings and steadings altered and enlarged as a result of generations of sound and successful farming. Generally speaking, the larger and richer the estate, the more substantial and uniform were its farmsteads, but varying from estate to estate, and from one branch of farming to another, these solidly functional buildings show many subtle variations on a theme. Partly serving the laird's own larder, the large home or mains (from 'demesne') farm was often the exemplar for the rest.

**Estate cottages,
Ardwell**

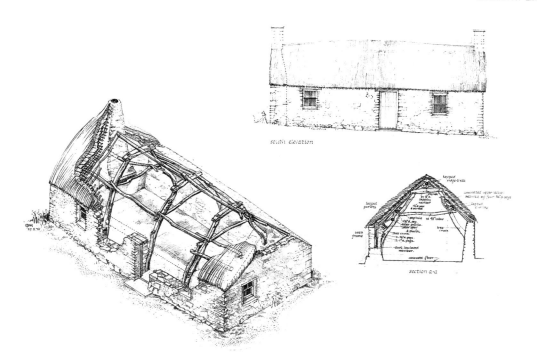

south elevation

section a-a

**Cottage,
Torthorwald:
isometric drawing
showing crucks
by GD Hay**

18 Torthorwald, Cottage

c AD 1800.

NY 032784. On the W side of the minor road running N from the A 709.

Founded as a burgh of barony in 1473, Torthorwald has all the attributes of a medieval village settlement: a castle, a parish church, water-supply for a millstead, and good cultivable ground which drains naturally down to the edge of the Lochar Moss. However, except for the castle, all the built elements of the village have been transformed since the late 18th century. The single-storeyed thatched cottage at NY 032784 dates from this period but, despite its date, it represents a valuable link with building customs of the medieval tenantry in this area.

The cottage is the last complete survivor of a once-strong cruck-framing tradition around Dumfries. The straw thatch, which has been renewed from time to time, and the irregular bulges of its boulder-stone footings give an external hint of its construction. One of the advantages of cruck-framing was that the side-walls, whether of mud, clay, turf, or inferior rubble, were merely for cladding and not for load-bearing; the weight of

the roof was borne by the crucks, generally springing from around ground-level. Their strength was determined by the quality of timber, their design, spacing and jointing. In turn, the resultant span and bay-lengths governed the dimensions and layout of the house itself.

In this building there are three oak cruck trusses of almost natural tree-trunk form, each pair joined together by an intermediate collar, and tenoned into the underside of a stout capping block. Longitudinal members (purlins) and closely spaced branch-rafters have been laid over this frame, and turf provides groundwork for the thatch. The interior once had a kitchen ('but') at the western end, and a ('ben') room at the other; in the middle was a small closet. Until recently there was a clay-coated and canopied chimney bracketed from the wall at the kitchen end; it was associated with a thatched cowl in place of a chimney stack.

Until 1948 an almost identical cottage stood a short distance to the south-east, its position now marked by a plaque in the roadside wall. This had been the boyhood home of the Reverend John Paton, missionary to the New Hebrides, whose parents moved here in 1830. When he returned to the village in 1885 he found only five thatched cottages, estimating that sixty or seventy had been removed or rebuilt since his childhood. Most of these, if not all, were probably cruck-framed. He also recorded the significant fact 'that the walls [of his parents' cottage] are quite modern, having all been rebuilt in my father's time [d. 1868], except only the few great foundation boulders piled around the oaken couples'.

Exactly where all the 'oaken couples' came from is not known. The village had been part of the Queensberry estate since 1622, but the tenants of Torthorwald do not appear to have been specially favoured with supplies of building timber from the oak woods with which Nithsdale was so well endowed. They probably had to make do with what they could find themselves. In the late 18th century oak, fir, birch and hazel trees were frequently dug up in the nearby Lochar Moss; according to a contemporary account, 'several of these trees are very large and fresh, and are applied by carpenters to various purposes of their trade'.

date from the last phases of occupation prior to the abandonment of the site in the early 19th century. The most substantial buildings are a mill and an inn, the latter standing close to the old Kirkcudbright—Ayrshire pack road. At the centre of the township there is an irregular pattern of enclosed fields, and much of the surrounding ground bears the tell-tale corrugations of old ploughing or rig-cultivation. Associated with these arable plots are the remains of no less than five corn-drying kilns. The drystone rubble foundations of the other buildings have few diagnostic features; one at least has a low-level byre drain, and some may have served as byre-dwellings.

---

20 Priorslynn Farm, Canonbie

c AD 1800.

NX 394759. Situated above farm at the S end of the village; call at farmhouse before visit.

On the terrace above this farmstead there is a long rectangular building with walls of clay and a corrugated iron roof (replacing thatch); inside, it is divided into two compartments and has five cruck trusses. The clay walls, which have been patched with masonry and brick, are set on stone footings and have been built in thin courses between layers of straw. The basic form of the oak crucks is similar to that of the cottage at Torthorwald (no. 18), but they are bigger and better finished. They consist of single blades joined by a collar-beam and tenoned into a stout capping member at the apex; the northernmost pair of blades has been sawn from the same trunk to form complementary half-tree sections.

The building probably dates from a period around 1800 when the Buccleuch estate was issuing regulations against the use of timber 'except for buildings that are to be erected in a substantial manner and covered with slates'. Clay building had long been a common feature in Canonbie. In 1772 the traveller, Thomas Pennant, noted that 'most part of the houses are built with clay', and described communal building practices similar to those at Dornock.

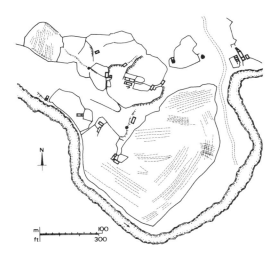

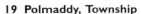

Polmaddy township: plan

---

19 Polmaddy, Township

18th and 19th centuries AD.

NX 589878. On the edge of Dundeugh Forest of the A 713; cross the Polmaddy Burn by footbridge.

It is likely that Polmaddy was a joint tenancy farm and, although on record from the early 16th century, most of the surviving remains probably

Clay building, Priorslynn Farm

21* Ellisland Farm

Late 18th century AD.

NX 929838. At end of track on E side of A 76.

In 1788 Robert Burns took up farming at this small 170-acre (68.8 ha) tenancy on the Dalswinton estate situated on the banks of the River Nith, 1.25 km downstream from Friars' Carse. With financial assistance from the laird, Patrick Miller, who was a keen agricultural improver, Burns had some fields enclosed, and the farmhouse built by Thomas Boyd, a local architect and builder (see nos 4, 23). But the farm proved better suited to the creation of poetry than profit, and in 1791 Burns managed to release himself from the tenancy and what he called 'a ruinous affair' to concentrate on his job as Excise officer. Alongside personal and literary items relating to the poet, the single-storeyed farmhouse retains some original fittings, including an oven and part of a kitchen range installed by Burns. The granary has also been refurbished as a museum of farming life.

Clay building, Priorslynn Farm: interior showing cruck construction
(Left)

COUNTRY HOUSES 5 AND GARDENS

Cally Palace Hotel

At the hub of the estate was the laird's own residence. Even if only one of a number possessed by a single, widely ramified family, the great house usually reflected the owner's success in running his estates, his business (perhaps in the cities or colonies), and in the marriage stakes. The architecture and furnishings of these mansions thus represent episodes when a family chose to rehouse itself in a style and on a scale suited to its circumstances and its ideals. Some houses underwent such upheavals regularly, especially on changes of ownership, and in the 19th century the pressure to enlarge or rebuild must have been almost irresistible. Nevertheless, not every family, nor every generation of an architecturally conscious family, was motivated to build anew; whether born of contentment or economic necessity, conservatism is just as strong as innovation in the history of domestic architecture in Dumfries and Galloway. Both traits are manifest in the design of Drumlanrig Castle (no. 25). By the time of its completion in 1690 Drumlanrig's Renaissance palace layout was at least three generations out of fashion, but its great show-front was a brave attempt at completely up-to-date Classicism. Drumlanrig grew over and around an older building on the same site, and many houses of lesser rank incorporate similar evidence of continuity from earlier centuries.

By national standards the region is by no means richly endowed with mansion houses, but present numbers are deceptive. The lost or derelict mansions of Dumfries and Galloway include Balgreggan House (NX 087503; William Adam, architect, *c* 1725-30), Barholm House

(NX 471592; Robert Adam, *c* 1790), Glasserton House (NX 4137; John Baxter, 1740-1), Langholm Lodge (NY 3585; James Playfair, 1787), Gelston Castle (NX 777583), Terregles House (NX 933778) and Jardine Hall (NY 0987; last remodelled 1894-7). Furthermore, houses which received large 19th-century additions have since been pruned to more manageable proportions, none to better effect than Logan House (NX 096428), where demolition of 1874 additions revealed an attractive mid 18th-century core. Most illusory of all are the houses that never were, those design-drawings which, like Robert Adam's Castle Stewart (1787), never materialised into buildings on the ground. William Adam had no less than five aborted projects within the region.

Fortunately, William's distinctively robust brand of Classicism still survives at the private houses of Craigdarroch (NX 742909; 1726-9 and later) and Tinwald (NY 017803; 1738-40, interior rebuilt 1946-8), which he executed with advice from his mentor, Sir John Clerk of Penicuik. One of William Adam's contemporaries was John Baxter, an Edinburgh mason-architect who also looked to Clerk for advice and patronage. Baxter began work in 1740 on both Glasserton House and Galloway House (no. 24), the two biggest commissions of his career, obviously benefiting from the influence and experience of Sir John, who was brother-in-law of James, 5th Earl of Galloway, rebuilder of Glasserton and uncle of Lord Garlies, builder of Galloway House.

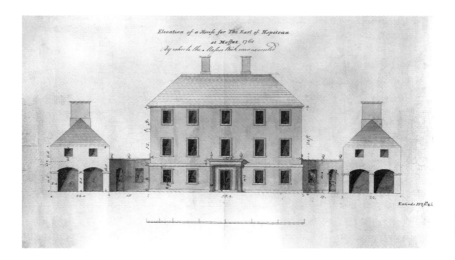

Moffat House Hotel

Work by William Adam's distinguished sons is represented by Moffat House (NT 083053; now a hotel) and Kirkdale House (NX 515533; a private residence), although there are many unauthenticated 'Adam-style' derivatives. Moffat House was built *c* 1761-2 for the 2nd Earl of Hopetoun to the designs of William's eldest son, John. It comprises a three-storeyed main block with two-storeyed pavilions. The plain formality of the layout is warmed by the textured effect of the neat rubble masonry and ashlar dressings, the stonework and the loftiness of the main block giving the ensemble a homely and old-fashioned air. Within, the only original feature of note is an open-well geometric stair.

Kirkdale House

With its clinically severe lines, sharpened by the use of grey granite ashlar masonry, the exterior of Robert Adam's Kirkdale is the very opposite of homeliness and warmth. Erected in 1787-8 for Sir Samuel Hannay, one of Galloway's enterprising merchant-lairds, Kirkdale bears the hallmarks of Adam's mature neo-Classical style, and on this sloping site the house and its flanking pavilions are displayed to good effect both at the rear and at the front. The interior of the four-storeyed central block had to be reconstructed after a fire in 1890. Adam's other work for his Hannay patron included the bridge at the entrance to the house, and almost certainly the octagonal stables-block further up the hill at NX 512536.

Credit for the most notable Classical house in the region, however, goes not to the Adam family, but to Robert Mylne, descendant of an equally famous and even longer line of masons and architects. Whilst engaged on his celebrated scheme for the first Blackfriars Bridge in London, the young architect put into effect the designs for Cally (no. 23) which he first submitted in 1759.

Endowed with all the authority of fully developed Georgian mansions, Galloway House and Cally assume the leading roles in the 18th-century stage set, but the region has a full supporting cast of classic houses of the middle size. The type is exemplified by Knockhill House (NY 165740; 1777, private residence), where an inscription above the porch, freely adapting the words of Abraham Cowley, proclaims it to be 'Too Small for Envy, for Contempt too Great'. Notions of symmetrical planning were also applied to lesser lairds' houses and farmhouses, providing the basis of standard farmhouse design in the 19th century. The 1721 addition to Hills Castle (NX 912726), Ross Mains (NY 067887; 1728) and Glen (NX 547579; founded 1734) mark early dated stages in this process.

Knockhill House

It is possible that Lochryan House (NX 065688; private residence), built for Colonel Agnew of Croach (Lochryan) after 1701, was the first in the local series of symmetrically planned lairds' houses. However, the exterior is quite unlike any other in Scotland, and the castellated roof-line is unlikely to be original. The first of the region's mansions of Romantic castellated design was the Adam-style castle at Raehills (NY 063943), which Alexander Stevens, an Edinburgh architect, produced for the 3rd Earl of Hopetoun in 1786. This was considerably enlarged and altered between 1828 and 1834, but Stevens' original design is still preserved in the shape of a wooden model at Raehills.

The most notable of the few houses of ecclesiastical Gothic style is Hensol (NX 675698), designed for John Cunningham in about 1825 by Robert Lugar, the English architect who had created the earliest asymmetrical Gothic houses in Scotland. Wrought in rock-faced granite masonry, the design of Hensol is loosely based on English Tudor Gothic forms, as was Cumstoun (NX 684535) when first built in 1827-9 for Adam Maitland of Dundrennan. The designer of this first phase of Cumstoun was Thomas Hamilton, one of the major Edinburgh architects of the period and a great exponent of Greek Revival styles.

Edinburgh, the 'Athens of the North', was the principal setting in Scotland for Greek Revival architecture, but two Dumfriesshire houses stand at the forefront of this movement. Kinmount (NY 140687), built in 1812 for the 5th Marquess of Queensberry, was Robert Smirke's first essay in his influential 'Graeco-Cubist' style, a deliberately severe composition of interpenetrating blocks centred upon a lantern-towered saloon. Smirke entrusted this commission to a young pupil, William Burn, then at the threshold of a long and outstanding architectural career. Kinmount was Burn's earliest major charge, and the elegant villa at Craigielands (NT 076017; 1817) was his first known wholly Grecian house. Its lanterned cross-plan hall was obviously derived from Kinmount, but Craigielands itself then served as a model for many other Scottish 'Greek' mansions of the middle size.

It was Burn's own pupil, David Bryce, who carried the torch for his master in the development of country house styles, especially the vogue for 'Scottish Baronial' which received a full repertory of motifs upon the publication of R W Billings' *Baronial and Ecclesiastical Antiquities of Scotland* (1845-52). By that time, Bryce was well into his stride, and at Shambellie (no. 22), Capenoch (NX 843938; additions and alterations 1847, 1854-6, 1868), and Castlemilk (NY 149775; 1863-4) he found patrons wishing to indulge in this stirring evocation of Scotland's past. Castlemilk, once a centre of genuine medieval lordship, is regarded as 'one of the largest and most lavish of Bryce's great Baronial houses', and all his domestic work displays the solid craftsmanship and comforts of mid-Victorian Scotland.

Craigcleuch (Scottish Explorers' Museum)

Lochinch Castle

Visitors to the Scottish Explorers' Museum at Craigcleuch (NY 343869) will find that it is housed in a building of 'Jacobethan' (Elizabethan/Jacobean) style. The Victorian fortalice of Threave House (NX 753603; 1871) can be seen from Threave Gardens (NTS) and at the end of the circuit through Castle Kennedy Gardens (no. 26) is the grandiose Lochinch Castle (NX 107618), which was designed for the 10th Earl of Stair in 1864-7 by the Edinburgh firm of Brown and Wardrop. It is probably the region's biggest Scottish Baronial mansion on public display, although it is not open to the public.

Many of the last country houses were belittled by contemporary hotels such as the Baronial-style hotel which stands dominant on the North Cliff at Portpatrick (NW 997543; James Kennedy Hunter, architect, 1902-3, enlarged 1905-6), its qualities as a fairy-tale castle probably much enhanced upon the introduction of locally generated electric lighting in 1905. The hotel and the electricity were initiated by Charles Orr Ewing who had acquired the Dunskey estate in 1898 and rebuilt Dunskey House (NX 000559; James Kennedy Hunter, architect, 1903). In its own slightly rambling manner this building marks a last tribute to the Baronial style in Galloway.

Portpatrick Hotel

The last word, as always, rests with the owner, not the architect. To Sir Herbert Maxwell of Monreith in 1932 'no change in the equipment of country houses ... has been more general than the provision of bathrooms. Tubs in bedrooms of course were always provided; but if the luxury of a hot bath were required (it was deemed effeminate and enfeebling except in case of illness), cans of hot water had to be carried laboriously up many flights of stairs ...' One of Sir Herbert's grandsons was Gavin Maxwell, well-known naturalist and author, and to him, Monreith House (NX 356428; Alexander Stevens, architect, 1791) had 'the fusty Victorian aura of dark wall paint and damp-stained bedroom ceilings'. Here, his grandfather 'passed his old age between his gardens and the study he had built for himself at the end of a long corridor. At the far side of this incredibly untidy room ... he would sit at a big desk between two atrocious stained-glass windows ...'.

For most owners, including Sir Herbert Maxwell, author of a book on Scottish gardens, the setting and 'prospect' of a country house was just as important as the architectural design itself. Whilst the region cannot claim any early gardens, its mild climate has been conducive to the survival and revival of some notable creations of 18th century and later date. The gardens established by Andrew Heron in his 'little paradise' at Bargaly (NX 4666) and noted by Sir John Clerk in 1721 are now just a matter of astonishing historical record: 'He had grapes and figs of several sorts, 38 kinds of cherries, 40 of plums, near 80 kinds of apples and as many pears'. Sir John had found the formal gardens at Drumlanrig (no. 25) 'by far the finest in the kingdom'. These gardens survived a period of neglect and partial destruction in the later 18th century to be restored almost to their former glory.

Monreith House

A similar fate befell the region's most noteworthy historic garden which is at Castle Kennedy (no. 26). Its restoration was the last of four commissions in Galloway entrusted to the distinguished architect and landscape gardener, John Claudius Loudon. His plans for Mabie (NX 950708; now forestry) never materialised, while those carried out at Castlewigg (NX 427432) and Barnbarroch (NX 398515) have descended to a completely natural state, and the houses are in ruins. At Barnbarroch his drawings were also used for remodelling the house, and his designs for the surrounding picturesque garden with its vista of lake, waterfall and woods look like a worthy reflection of his talents.

Shambellie House: perspective of south front by David Bryce, 1854

22* Shambellie House, New Abbey

AD 1856-7.

NX 960666. Off the A 710 N of New Abbey; signposted.

NMS, Museum of Costume.

Drawn to Shambellie by the collection of historic gowns and costumes, visitors will find that the house has much interest in its own right. Built in 1856-7 for William Stewart to the design of David Bryce, it is a small, virtually unaltered Victorian mansion of Scottish Baronial style. In its sylvan setting, Shambellie appears to be a typically solid and comfortable house suited to a Victorian landed gentleman of moderate means. It stands its ground as naturally as any minor Scottish laird's house of the late 16th or 17th century, whose details it imitates.

Yet, the placid and confident aura which surrounds the building could not be more deceptive. Its construction was a tale of acrimony, fuelled by the client's fastidious sense of economy. Rancour usually leaves much documentation in its trail, and Alistair Rowan has worked through a mass of evidence to produce a fascinating guide-booklet *The Creation of Shambellie* (1982). In his words, 'among Victorian country houses in Scotland, Shambellie is uniquely unfortunate in its building history. Almost everything that could go wrong with its construction did so. Mr Stewart fell out with his architect, the tradesmen he had employed, his friends and almost everybody connected with the house. In the end he was brought to court by his builder'.

The client's concern with cost manifested itself early. Bryce's scheme matched Mr Stewart's expectations, but the estimated £2,700-£2,800 was well beyond what he was prepared to pay. Bryce's perspective view shows Shambellie as it might have been, but the house was built on a reduced scale in accordance with a second set of plans prepared in 1855. The arrangement of the bay windows on the garden front remained unaltered, but the differences between the first design and the existing house represent the gap between Mr Stewart's dream and financial reality. The effects of economy are also visible within. As Professor Rowan points out, 'modest plaster cornices replace the ornate bracketed designs intended for the main rooms; embellishments in the masonry are omitted; deal is substituted for oak; the chimney-pieces are not by Bryce but by a jobbing mason from Carlisle; and finally, to achieve a saving of a few feet in the banisters, the main stair has been turned to run in the opposite direction to that which Bryce intended, a last-minute alteration that made the first floor pass clumsily across one of the windows of the entrance front'. To keep down costs the attics were also left unfinished and not fitted up until 1866. By this time Stewart calculated that the house had cost him just short of £3,000, a sum which he had initially considered to be beyond his means; on top of this he also had substantial legal payments to make. As his lawyer had sagely advised him in 1860 'Enlightened liberality in good time is real economy in the end'.

Cally Palace Hotel: central block

Cally Palace Hotel: lobby

23 Cally House (Cally Palace Hotel)

c AD 1759-65 and later.

NX 599549. Approached from E end of Gatehouse of Fleet; signposted.

The title of palace, though only recently conferred, well suits this stately neo-Classical mansion.

Designed and built between 1759 and 1765, it demonstrates tangibly the rise in the landed fortunes of the Murrays of Broughton. Marriage to a Lennox heiress brought the Cally estate into the possession of Richard Murray (d. 1690), and each of the next two generations married into the family of the Earls of Galloway, their near-neighbours in Wigtownshire. The mother of James Murray (d. 1799), builder of this mansion and Broughton House in Kirkcudbright (no. 14), was daughter of the 5th Earl, and his wife was his first cousin, daughter of the builder of Galloway House (no. 24).

No doubt affected by the activities of his in-laws, Alexander Murray (d. 1750) toyed with schemes for a new house and garden prepared by William Adam in about 1742; however, only the flanking pavilions were built, later to be removed. The recommendation of the youthful Robert Mylne as architect must have been made by James Murray's brother-in-law, Lord Garlies (later 7th Earl of Galloway); his role as intermediate patron is borne out by the fact that in 1759 Mylne's draft designs were sent from Rome to him, not direct to Murray.

Mylne's commentary shows the staffing requirements of a great house, and reflects the hierarchy of contemporary society. The lowest floor 'holds the kitchen and all the nauseous places that should not be seen or smelt by company'. On the ground floor, the main public rooms (a dining-parlour, grand dining- room, and drawing-room) were centred around a great hall. The bedrooms were on the first floor, the nursery and some guest bedrooms shared the second floor with the rooms of the principal servants, whilst the garrets were set aside 'for the lower servants'.

As was later claimed, the house was probably the first in southern Scotland to be built of granite ashlar masonry, probably from Kirkmabreck. The design was unusual in having a 1-2-2-1 rhythm in the fenestration, which disguises the effect of the broad 4-bay pedimented centrepiece. In 1794 the linking corridors and pavilions were raised one storey higher in harmonious style by a local architect, Thomas Boyd.

The most substantial alterations, however, were those executed in 1833-7 for James Murray's

natural son, Alexander. The architect was John Buonarotti Papworth, who was also employed by Murray of Broughton at Killybegs in County Donegal. The portico and marble lobby which he added to the front of Cally excited much comment; William Henry Playfair was impressed, but Lord Cockburn was 'disappointed ... The marble lobby is new in Scotland, and beautiful. But for a thing of the kind, it is too little and far too fine for a mere common lobby ... The factor told me that the whole marble of this lobby was cut, and polished, and put up by a common workman from Whitehaven'. He later recanted, declaring that 'on the whole, it is a beautiful portico; and Papworth's taste may be observed in all the internal details'.

Even Lord Cockburn was prepared to admit to the beautiful natural setting of the house, 'one of the finest in Scotland'. Work on the pleasure grounds in about 1788 included the building of a small two-storeyed garden pavilion in the form of a Gothic temple, which now stands ruinous in forest plantation (NX 606543). In addition to a walled garden, there were extensive orchards, and, about 1 km south of the mansion, a well-stocked deer park (NX 5953). The landscaped policies were planted with trees. According to Robert Heron in 1792, 'Every deformity within these grounds is concealed, or converted into beauty by wood'. However, Loudon found the trees 'in many places too formal and unconnected'. More fundamentally, he declared the house to be incorrectly aligned: 'the entrance front is on the wrong side, and none of the windows of the principal rooms look towards the river'. To a professional, nothing can ever be quite perfect!

24 Galloway House

c AD 1740-5 and later.

NX 478452. Signposted at the W end of Garlieston village.

Galloway House is the greatest residence built for the Stewart family of Garlies, entitled Lords Garlies from 1607 and Earls of Galloway after 1623. It was built c 1740-5 for Lord Garlies, son of the 5th Earl of Galloway; the basic designs were those of John Douglas amended by John Baxter in association with Sir John Clerk of Penicuik. Its appearance suffered partly because of compromises made in the course of its creation, but Art's loss is History's gain; the building of Galloway House gives an insight into a tense relationship between client, architect and builder.

The little that is known of Douglas's career appears to cast doubt on his talent and personal integrity. But, although prepared to accept Baxter as building-contractor, Lord Garlies was attached to Douglas's 'notion of a little house'; 'dark passages nor dark entries will give me no uneasiness'. He could afford no more than £2,000 to build and furnish the house, but, faced with a Baxter-Clerk plan for a modest villa, Garlies remained adamant in his desire for a four-storeyed frontage and a three-bay centrepiece, and found economies elsewhere. Acting under his instructions, Baxter was obliged to take out 24 windows and to reduce the second storey to a height of only 3 m.

The nucleus of the house as existing consists of a four-storeyed main block linked to a pair of three-storeyed frontal pavilions. The walls are of whinstone with red sandstone dressings, balancing warmth and tradition against refinement and grandeur. But there is a heavy-handedness in the design which emanates from the scale and proportions of the three-bay pedimented centrepiece. Later additions have added to the ponderous effect. In 1842 William Burn prepared a scheme for the 9th Earl which involved the addition of upper storeys to the pavilions and wing-walls, and sizeable infill sections built to the same height as the main block. Too large for the earl's descendants, the house was sold in 1907, and in 1909-10 the new owner commissioned Robert

Cally Palace Hotel:
plasterwork detail
(Left)

Galloway House

**Galloway House:
entrance hall**
(Right)

Lorimer to remodel the interior. His re-designed and enlarged hall is now probably the most elegant feature of the house.

It was near Clary that Lord Garlies had first thought of building the new family seat, but by 1737 his choice was Pouton, 'the healthiest, pleasantest, most agreeable and convenient place in the whole estate'. Just what financial arrangements permitted the son to commence building here in the same year as his father began again at Glasserton is not recorded, but it is clear that money was in short supply throughout the building campaign.

Lack of finance probably also restricted early development of the gardens and policies. It was the 7th Earl (d. 1806), a great student of arboriculture and silviculture, who contributed most to the landscaping of the park and the improvement of the estate. In 1791 it was said that 'Under his care trees grow on every exposure; and every species of them thrive as well about Galloway House as in any part of England ... His Lordship's designs are great; and he is accomplishing them by planting at the rate of 200,000 trees every year'. The park and gardens were redesigned in about 1850, but the splendid trees in this neighbourhood are a worthy legacy of the 7th Earl.

The nearby village of Garlieston was also his creation. Founded principally as a fishing-station, it developed into a trading port with supporting marine industries. By the 1790s, thanks largely to the 7th Earl, Galloway House stood in a developing landscape: 'from its windows are seen the richest fields, an indented coast, adorned with growing improvements ... The principal rooms are spacious,

and the library is stored with many thousand valuable volumes'. What better image of the noble life in the Age of Improvement?

25* Drumlanrig Castle

AD 1679-c 1690.

NX 851992. Well signposted on the A76, N of Dumfries, and on all major routes.

This grand mansion stands upon a terraced platform among the woods of upper Nithsdale, its four-square turreted profile and pink-coloured sandstone contrasting with the greenery of its surroundings. Completed in about 1690, Drumlanrig became the home of James Douglas, 2nd Duke of Queensberry, known as the 'Union Duke' because of his role in the Treaty of Union of 1707. During these negotiations Daniel Defoe acted for Harley of Queen Anne's government; at Drumlanrig he was impressed by 'a palace so glorious, gardens so fine, and everything so truly magnificent ... all in a wild, mountainous country, the like we had not seen before', but which in some respects reminded him of Derbyshire.

The builder of this noble pile was James's father, William, 3rd Earl and (from 1684) 1st Duke of Queensberry; he died in 1695 ruined, it is said, by the expense it had incurred. The design that he adopted in 1679 was basically one that had been presented to his grandfather in 1618. The layout followed that of Heriot's Hospital, Edinburgh, and was probably by the same accomplished mason-architect, William Wallace. By 1679, however, Classicism was the order of the day. The central part of the entrance front thus has two storeys of pedimented windows framed within pilasters of a giant Corinthian Order; a central projecting entrance-porch is similarly treated, and rises to a clock-lantern which wears a ducal coronet. The entry is on a terrace above an arcaded basement, and is approached by a double circular staircase.

The architect was almost certainly James Smith, who had been a mason at Holyroodhouse under Sir William Bruce and Robert Mylne (d. 1710). In 1683, during the Drumlanrig campaign and on the recommendation of the earl, he was appointed Overseer of the Royal Works in Scotland in succession to Bruce. It is thus not surprising that Drumlanrig's frontispiece should owe much to Bruce's west front at Holyroodhouse, and that in his first known design Smith should be uncertain in his handling of the elements of Classical architecture. However, the seeds of his architectural career may have been sown during earlier travels in Italy, and this may simply be the faltering first step of the father of British Palladianism. The Master of Works was William Lukup, who is represented with the tools of his trade on a carved headstone of 1685 in Durisdeer churchyard (no. 62).

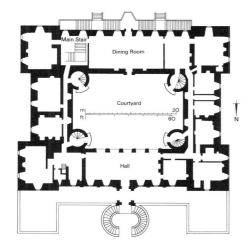

Drumlanrig Castle: first-floor plan (Left)

Drumlanrig Castle: entrance front

Externally homogeneous, parts of the structure, especially the thick-walled eastern quarter, probably incorporate much of the old medieval castle, which by 1618 had assumed an irregular quadrangular layout. James Douglas (d. 1578) is credited with its completion in this form, but its origins probably go back beyond 1429 when the castle first comes on record. The barony itself was in the possession of the Douglases from about 1357 until 1810, when upon the death of the 4th Duke, the title and most of the estates passed to the 3rd Duke of Buccleuch, grandson of Lady Jane Douglas, daughter of the 'Union Duke'.

Drumlanrig Castle: entrance front

Drumlanrig Castle: vaulted basement beneath terrace

The succession of the Scotts of Buccleuch marks a watershed in the history of Drumlanrig, for the 3rd Duke's descendants (especially the 5th Duke, the 7th Duke of Queensberry, d. 1884) carried out much-needed programmes of restoration, giving the house the careful treatment normally accorded an old master. Service wings were added on each side of the forecourt and were designed with restraint and sympathy, probably by William Burn who came to enjoy much patronage from the 5th Duke at his other properties.

Also thanks to the Buccleuchs, the contents of Drumlanrig have become a veritable 'treasure house', representing parts of three family collections with imports from former residences elsewhere; Rembrandt's masterpiece, 'An Old Woman Reading' (1655), must be one of the more prized items. Imported plenishings include at least one carved overmantel by the celebrated Grinling Gibbons. Most of the wood carving and panelling was installed in existing positions in the 1930s.

An inventory of 1694 describes the internal arrangements and fittings of the newly completed mansion. The main entrance was then on the inner face of the south range, reached through an open arcade in the north range, now the front hall. At this level the south range had a 'low' dining-room, later enlarged, and a drawing-room, later converted to a serving-room. Vertical circulation was only by the newel stairs in the re-entrant angles of the courtyard, but the open-well wooden staircase was completed shortly afterwards in 1697. The great drawing-room on the first floor of the south range was originally the state dining-room, the ante-room on the west having been the principal drawing-room; the adjacent room, where Bonnie Prince Charlie slept in December 1745, still possesses the painted overmantel described in 1694 as 'ye history of Hercules and ye dragon'.

Great formal gardens were laid out as a fitting complement to the house. On the south front there are original staircases with scrolled wrought-iron balustrades, and the landing of the main double stair stands above a columned pavilion. In 1721 Sir John Clerk was much impressed by the gardens, 'excellently laid out in the newest fashion with parterres, terraces, sloping banks, wildernesses, hedges, water works, etc., and the Duke keeps daily at work a gardener and 26 men to dress them'. The 3rd Duke of Queensberry created a lake and a cascade, and busied himself with tree planting. By 1772 Drumlanrig had become embosomed in trees', and the ascent to it was through a fine and well-planted park'.

Unfortunately, in 1786 the trees were devastated 'by an uncommonly high wind', and then by the 4th Duke, who had almost the whole of the surrounding woodlands cut down. Tree planting recommenced after 1810, and great progress with the formal gardens was made in the 1830s when they were laid out in accordance with the pattern shown on old drawings. A few years later the parish minister was able to write that 'every facility is afforded to strangers to gratify their curiosity here [ie. in the greenhouses and vegetable garden], or in the lovely flower gardens in the immediate vicinity of the castle'.

26* Castle Kennedy, Gardens
18th and 19th centuries AD.

NX 1060, 1161, 1061. Well signposted on the A 75, E of Stranraer.

There have been records of garden designs and maintenance here since 1722. The earliest schemes were those of the architect, William Adam, perhaps in association with the Edinburgh nurseryman, William Boutcher senior. Adam took advantage of the peninsular setting and the irregular outline of the White and Black Lochs to blend the natural and the formal, the formal elements including an impressive canal between the lochs.

A peculiarity was that the gardens were laid out for the Earls of Stair at vast expense with no accompanying house, an unusual circumstance for Adam who normally arrived at garden design through architecture. From 1721 until 1867 the earls' local residence was Culhorn; Castle Kennedy (no.28) remained unrestored after a fire in 1716. A garden temple or pavilion was designed by Adam in about 1725 and was intended to be placed 'at the end of the bowling green', but it is doubtful whether it was ever built. The military campaigns of Adam's patron, the 2nd Earl of Stair (d. 1747), were commemorated by garden features still known as Mount Marlborough and Dettingen Avenue.

Mansion-less, the gardens continued to be carefully tended until about 1800, when, according to a report of 1832, that part of the garden 'called The Wilderness, in which there were various grass walks, regularly mown, some clumps of laurels, ornamental wood and hedges ... 'was, on the orders of the Earl of Stair, cut, disposed of ... thrown open and the intersecting hedges destroyed'. In 1841-2 the 8th Earl commissioned Loudon to restore the gardens. As a result of the discovery of a working copy of Adam's garden plan, rather more of the original scheme was revived than might otherwise have been expected.

The building of Lochinch Castle in 1867 led to the creation of surrounding formal gardens, including the sunken garden whose layout of flower-beds has been much simplified over the years.

Castle Kennedy Gardens (Left)

CASTLES AND TOWERS 6

Orchardton Castle

In the Middle Ages the exercise of lordship over men and lands was centred upon castles, towers, and 'manor places', the equivalents of the mansions, villas, and estate buildings described in preceding chapters. The period at which landowning families chose to abandon or remodel their old abodes— and life-styles—varied according to circumstance. The earliest 'modern' houses in the region are probably those of 1631 at Amisfield (NX 992838), and the 1634 building erected by the 1st Earl of Nithsdale within Caerlaverock Castle (no. 41). Not until the 18th century, however, did the majority of the region's lairds begin to provide for themselves houses which seem to us to be wholly domestic in appearance and arrangement.

There remained, however, a lingering respect for the stout qualities of the older buildings and their settings, even though, as Colly Cibber pointed out in *The Double Gallant* (1707), 'Old houses mended/Cost little less than new before they're ended'. Nevertheless, examples of such continuity are to be seen throughout the region, clearer and in greater numbers than in many other parts of Scotland. As we have seen, substantial medieval remains are enveloped within the fabric of Drumlanrig Castle (no. 25). Elsewhere, the evidence is less disguised, usually in the form of later extensions (eg nos 27, 31, 32, 37, and formerly 29 and 30). Hills Castle (NX 912726; private residence) is a 16th-century tower to which a house was attached in 1721; Kirkconnell House (NX 979680; private residence) and Amisfield are also good developed specimens. At Amisfield the upperworks of the 16th-century tower were further elaborated in about 1600, and in the late 1830s a pedimented villa was planted on to the front of the detached three-storeyed south range of 1631.

**Amisfield Castle
and House, by
Francis Grose,
1789**

Maxwelton House

Maxwelton House (NX 822897) and Lochnaw Castle (NW 991628) are
houses of this transformed kind open to the public. Maxwelton is a
modernised house of 17th-century and possibly earlier origin; it was in the
possession of the Earls of Glencairn until 1611, and the Lauries of
Maxwelton until 1966, one of its former residents being 'bonnie' Annie
Laurie, subject of the celebrated love song. Lochnaw Castle, ancestral home
of the Agnews, one-time hereditary sheriffs of Galloway, was massively
enlarged in two stages in the early 19th century, but now stands reduced to
its nucleus, an early 16th-century oblong tower with adjacent dwelling
ranges of 1663. A fragment of its predecessor occupies an island site in the
nearby loch.

Many medieval castles and towers, however, were simply abandoned to
their fate, some to be saved by modern works of restoration. No less than
ten castles in the region are now in the custody of Historic Scotland, and
others are under careful surveillance. The attention is well merited, for,
collectively, Dumfries and Galloway boasts the densest distribution in the
country of early earth-and-timber castles (mottes), and has an impressive
number of tower houses. Individually, too, the Motte of Urr (no. 44),
Caerlaverock Castle (no. 41), and Threave Castle (no. 38), are of an
international standard in the three main categories of medieval castle-
mottes, courtyard castles and towers.

Lochnaw Castle, prior to demolition of 19th-century additions

At the latest count almost one-quarter of known mottes in Scotland, 74 out of 317, are to be found in the south-west. The thick scatter in Annandale and Nithsdale appears to correspond with a tenurial structure of relatively small baronial fiefs of the 12th and 13th centuries. Annan (NY 192666) itself represents the earliest centre of the great feudal holding conferred on the incoming Bruce family in 1124, later to be transferred to Lochmaben (no. 42). The mottes of Galloway probably reflect a similar pattern of feudal settlement, but their numbers go well beyond what is known from scarce historical record (eg no. 43). Furthermore, 12th-century Galloway was a semi-independent principality, and many of the mottes probably originated in military campaigns. After mounting at least three expeditions, King Malcolm IV (1153-65) placed the province under military occupation, but in 1174 the Galwegians 'expelled ... all the bailiffs and guards whom the King of Scots had set over them ... and all the defences and castles which the King of Scots had established in their land they besieged, captured and destroyed'. The first Anglo-Norman settlers appear on record in this period and are associated with lands where mottes can still be found, eg Boreland of Borgue (NX 646517), Urr (no. 44), Anwoth (NX 585566), and New Abbey (NX 982651). A significant proportion of these incomers had ties with Cumbria.

A second phase of motte-building was promoted after 1185, not by the king, but by Roland, Lord of Galloway, who had ruthlessly reunified the divided lordship, having evidently slain the most powerful men, occupied their lands, and, following earlier royal example, 'in them he built castles and very many fortresses'. Distinguishing native imitations from genuine Anglo-Norman products is not easy. Indeed, the mottes of Galloway pose far more questions than answers to problems of feudal geography. Only part of one of them (no. 44) has been the subject of modern archaeological excavation, so the testimony of these ubiquitous giant earth-castles remains, tantalisingly, buried and mute.

The earth-shifting and general 'navvying' required to put up a motte should not be underestimated, but castles of stone and lime were vastly more expensive and time-consuming to build. It was through the richer nobles of the 13th century that such strongholds were introduced into the region, and at Buittle (NX 819616) and Cruggleton (NX 484428), traditional centres of Galloway lordship, stone castles were shaped out of older fortifications by the successors to Alan, last native lord of Galloway (d. 1234). Buittle came into the possession of the Balliol family, heirs to much of eastern Galloway through marriage to Alan's third daughter, Dervorguilla. During her widowhood (1268-90), Dervorguilla spent much time at Buittle, and it was from there in 1282 that she formulated and sealed the Statutes of Balliol College, Oxford. The castle itself occupies an extensive low-lying site on a bank of the River Urr. The surrounding ditches and stone defences, including the remains of a substantial gatehouse, are, however, shrouded in vegetation. Excavations at the promontory fortification of Cruggleton have shown that it too entered a stone-built phase in the later 13th century, probably at the hands of John Comyn, Earl of Buchan, descendant of one of the other Galloway co-heiresses.

The partition of the Galloway lordship was effected with royal support. Direct royal authority in the province was established through the sheriffdoms and castles at Wigtown (NX 438550; only slight earthwork traces) and Kirkcudbright (no. 40), the foundations of which suggest a courtyard castle of Edwardian design.

Near-contemporary baronial strongholds at Tibbers (NX 862982; 1298) and Auchencass (NT 063035) show similar English influences in their angle-towered, quadrangular layouts; indeed, Edward I is known to have stayed at Tibbers and to have assisted in its repair. Caerlaverock Castle (no. 41) may also have been an Anglo-Scottish product in the late 13th century, but the actual builder and the source of its unusual triangular layout are not known for certain. Equally enigmatic is the hall and gatehouse block of Morton Castle (no. 39), which possesses some derivative Edwardian elements and probably dates from the latter half of the 14th century.

Lochmaben Castle (no. 42) is a tough unglamorous relic of the era of Anglo-Scottish conflict, the peel and stone castle reflecting its strategic importance. Although plundered for building stone (see no. 16) and then partly rebuilt in modern times, Sanquhar Castle (NX 785093) has been a substantial courtyard castle of baronial rank, developed in the later Middle Ages by the Crichton family. The outer ditches, the gatehouse range, and the restored tower-house are its most conspicuous features.

Conflict was endemic in the vicinity of the Anglo- Scottish Border until the Union of the Crowns in 1603. The requirements of national defence were organised around major strongholds such as Lochmaben, whilst lairds found their fortified houses a private refuge from, or a base for feuding and cattle-thieving. Colourful legend probably has a historical basis; the wealth of the Armstrongs, the Elliots, and especially the Grahams, was much augmented by money raised from ransoms and livestock thefts, largely at the expense of Northern English farmers. These ill-gotten proceeds may well have funded the building of numerous minor towers which had appeared by the late 16th century at the height of cattle- and sheep- rustling activities. However, of the 41 possible tower sites noted in a survey of

Eskdale and Ewesdale, only one, Gilnockie or Hollows Tower (NY 382785), probably a former Armstrong residence, survives virtually intact. Clearly seen from the A 7, this mid 16th-century tower displays an ornately corbelled parapet and a beacon-stance at the apex of the south gable.

Gilknockie (Hollows) Tower

The beacon-platform or caphouse was characteristic of a number of 16th-century towers in this area, and at Hoddom (no. 30) its use as a signalling system was linked to a watch tower on a nearby hill. Another architectural effect of cattle thieving was the provision of enclosures (barmkins) into which the goods and cattle of a laird and his tenants were to be brought 'in trublous tyme'. The Scottish Parliament in 1535 enjoined that barmkins should be the equivalent of about 18.3 m square with walls over 6 m high, and the laird to erect 'a tower in the same if he thinks it expedient'. A partly rebuilt barmkin of this type and size, complete with its gatehouse, is attached to mid 16th-century Hills Castle (NX 912726).

**Torthorwald
Castle, aerial view**

Usually associated with enclosures and ancillary buildings, and affording a balance between security and domesticity, the tower-house was the standard form of late medieval residence throughout the region. There are known remains of over 80, and they are still being rediscovered. Their distribution and character provide guides to the pattern of landownership, the wealth and ambition of a landholding family being crudely measureable by the date, size, and quality of their building works. As befitted a residence of the mighty Douglases, Threave Castle (no. 38) was the earliest and greatest of the region's towers, dating probably from the 1370s. Similarly, Hoddom Castle (no. 30) which is unusually massive for a tower of *c* 1568, well matches the authority and status of one branch of the Maxwell family who held sway in the 16th century. The towers are of every grade and type, and the visitor may judge for himself where a particular building—and its owner—stood in the social and tenurial hierarchy. There could scarcely be a greater contrast in size between, say, Threave and the cylindrical Orchardton (no. 34) one of a group which emerged following the break-up of the Douglas empire in 1455.

All towers were to some degree lofty symbols of authority over peasant communities where single-storeyed housing was the norm. To be in the stone tower 'bracket' was a mark of social and architectural achievement. At Lochwood Castle (no. 35), for example, a motte stands close to its 15th-century stone-built successor, demonstrating the continuous occupation of this site from the 12th century. Torthorwald Castle (NY 032872), a 14th-century tower with later alterations and additions, is also set within earthworks possibly inherited from an earth-and- timber predecessor. An English map or 'platte' of 1547 depicts the one-time tower of Castlemilk (c NY 1477) actually on top of a motte, presumably of earlier date. The tower is shown in sufficient detail to include its timber forestair or ladder to an upper doorway, a hint of a corbelled parapet, at least one barred window, and what might have been three gun-ports.

The defences of most castles and towers depended primarily on the natural strength of their positions. As elsewhere in Scotland, many castles occupied sites which were difficult to approach undetected, either because of their height, inaccessibility, or insularity, watery defences and amphibious life-styles being particularly apparent in this part of the world. However, the choice of sites was also governed by other considerations, including proximity to fertile agricultural land, or areas of profitable livestock farming, basic resources over which a castle occupant would wish to keep a watchful eye.

As can be seen in the buildings described below, man-made defences were of four main categories: outworks and enclosures to keep would-be assailants at a distance; special measures to protect vulnerable gateways and doorways; for close-range defence, arrow-slits and, later gun-ports; and, at the wall head, slots, battlements, and platforms, from which a 'drop on the head' form of defence could be conducted.

At Threave Castle (no. 38) the loopholed curtain-wall with circular angle-towers represents an early response to the threat of gunpowder artillery. Whether it was constructed in the early 1450s, as has been claimed, or in the late 15th century when Threave was in royal custody, it is likely to have been the first scheme of its kind in Scotland. Curiously, no other major stronghold in this frontier zone was converted into an artillery fortress, although most were liberally furnished with gun-ports. The only known artillery fortification of later design is the small redoubt on Burnswark Hill (no. 52), possibly a Scottish work of about 1648.

"Platte of Milkcastle", 1547

27 Rockhall Hotel

AD 1610 and later.

NX 056755. A hotel signposted from the A 75, E of Collin.

Although altered on at least four occasions, Rockhall Hotel is a perfectly genuine tower-house of early 17th-century origin. This is the building described in 1610 as 'the place of Rockhall lately built' by Sir William Grierson of Lag, one of whose descendants was a hated enemy of the Covenanters.

Its ancestry can be sensed immediately from its L-plan form and its three storeys. Closer examination reveals details that have been modified or dislocated in the course of its history. Originally, the main entrance was at the foot of the rounded turret in the angle, the present entrance dating from about 1915. The windows have been altered throughout, but the positions of original openings can still be detected by the relieving-arches which protected their lintels. The easternmost bay in the east wing is a well-disguised 18th-century addition, and a large window in the front wall occupies the position of an entrance-porch which stood here from about 1880 to 1915. The original upperworks have been ironed out with plain copes and later roofing. Inside, successive remodellings have left little obvious trace of the original layout, although part of the vaulted kitchen and service basement has survived intact.

28* Castle Kennedy

c AD 1607.

NX 110609. Signposted on the A 75, E of Stranraer.

The ruins of Castle Kennedy have been a sad monument to fire-damage ever since a fateful night in late October or early November 1716. A fire, lit to air the drawing room and supposedly put out by the maid before she went to bed, broke out again in the night, consuming almost everything except the occupants, three pictures, and the masonry we still see. Much attention was later lavished on the gardens (no. 26), but the shell of this burnt-out pile was left relatively undisturbed and unrestored.

The nucleus of the castle dates from the early 17th century when the Inch estate belonged to the Kennedy family, Earls of Cassillis, hence the name; building work was in progress in 1607. Temporarily in the possession of the Hamiltons of Bargany, Inch and other Wigtownshire properties were in 1677 acquired by the Dalrymples of Stair, another family of Ayrshire origin who came to acquire considerable political and military distinction. The house that they inherited comprised a five-storeyed central block with flanking turrets and towers, laid out symmetrically except for an off-centre entrance in the east wall. This led into a passage on the ground floor (formerly vaulted), and the main stair rose within an adjacent turret in the south re-entrant angle. The Dalrymples themselves added two-storeyed ranges to the north and west, probably in the early 18th century, and surviving inventories give a room-by-room list of the furnishings in 1698 and 1702, a poignant record of all that was lost in 1716.

29 Castle of Park

AD 1590.

NX 188571. The approach-track ascends from the W side of the curve in the A 75 W of Glenluce.

Seen and seeing for miles around, Castle of Park stands high on a tree-skirted platform above the Water of Luce, the very model of a late 16th-century Galloway laird's house. Now bereft of its 18th-century wings, but carefully restored to pristine condition, it rises abruptly from this plateau to four full storeys and a garret.

Castle of Park

The rooms in the main block are served by a stair in the projecting turret, giving it an overall L-plan form. Steeply pitched roofs over the main block and wing are independently constructed with crowstepped gables. There is no parapet, and corbelling, so beloved of tower-house builders, is restricted to a minor turret in the re-entrant angle. The lateral chimney-stack in the east side-wall serves a large hall fireplace, while the chunky stack above the north gable is related to a basement kitchen. Castle of Park is of an age when integrated service facilities were the norm.

The doorway is in the re-entrant angle, protected by the usual shot-hole. An inscribed panel above the entrance helpfully records that building work was begun on 1 March 1590 by Thomas Hay of Park and Janet McDowall, his wife. Thomas (d. 1628) was son of the last abbot of Glenluce Abbey (no. 72) and is reputed to have plundered the abbey for building-materials. The Hays, evidently descended from a minor branch of the Earls of Errol, held the lands of Park from the 16th century down to modern times. In 1870 it was reported that 'about forty years ago, everything portable was removed to Dunragit', another Hay residence.

The tower received later additions, which have been removed, but it remained virtually unaltered itself. The compact service arrangements on the ground floor consist of vaulted cellars and kitchen laid out *en suite* with linking corridor.

Castle of Park, prior to the demolition of the wings and re-harling

On the first floor, an indent in the wall immediately to the right of the entrance shows the likely position of a wooden screen at the 'lower' end of the great hall. At the other end, small chambers have been contrived on each side of the large intrusive kitchen stack; a similar pattern is repeated on the floors above. The main rooms on the second floor are paired with matching garderobes in the side-wall. The roof structure is basically original.

Hoddom Castle
(Top left and middle)

30 Hoddom Castle and Repentance Tower

16th century AD.

NY 155729, 155722. The castle grounds are a caravan park off the B 725; a footpath from the same road leads to the tower on the hill.

Towering over its courtyard, the huge mass of Hoddom Castle bears the scars, not of war, but of 19th-century additions lately demolished. However, long before the castellated additions of 1826-7 were ever thought of, this was a building which had seen real military action, having been vigorously attacked three times within the first few years of its existence. Replacing an older castle on the opposite bank of the river, Hoddom was built by John Maxwell, 4th Lord Herries, shortly before 1568 as his chief residential stronghold on the West March.

For its date this is a massive structure, standing to a height of over 21.3 m with walls 2.7 m thick at base. In conception it is akin to older generations of 'power houses' such as Comlongon (no. 37), but externally is distinguished from them in its liberal provision of gun-ports and in the decorative carved treatment of its corbelling and door-surround. Viewed from the caravan park, the later heightening of the turreted wing obscures the castle's highest original feature, a beacon platform corbelled out from the apex of the north gable. The purpose of this was explained in the Border Laws which enjoined that 'ever in war and in peace, the watch to be kept on the house-head; and in war the beacon in the fire-pan to be kept and never fail burning, so long as the Englishmen remain in Scotland; and with a bell to be on the head of the fire-pan which shall ring whenever the fray is, or that the watchman seeing the thieves disobedient come over the Water of Annan, or thereabouts, and knows them to be enemies'.

Repentance Tower (Left)

The platform at Hoddom is especially significant because it can be related, uniquely, to a watch tower which stands on the summit of Trailtrow Hill to the south. Compared to its parent in the valley below, this tower is a diminutive oblong structure of three main storeys, but from its vantage point commands a very extensive view of the lower reaches of the Annan and the Solway shore. It too was built by John Maxwell, 4th Lord Herries. 'REPENTENCE' is carved on the door lintel, possibly a token of regret for the fact that it was built out of the remains of a demolished chapel in whose burial-ground it stands.

It was evidently useful. In 1579 Maxwell recommended that 'the watch tower upon Trailtrow, called Repentance, must be mended of the little defacing the English army made of it [probably in 1570]; and ... the great bell and the fire-pan put on it ...'. The parapet was reconstructed in the early 18th century, and the upper floor fitted up as a dovecot, an unconscious symbol of peace and changed attitudes towards the Auld Enemy—or was it?

Drumcoltran Castle prior to partial demolition of house.

31* Drumcoltran Castle

16th century AD.

NX 869682. Signposted on the A 711, and situated about 2 km N of Kirkgunzeon village.

Historic Scotland.

Its domestic duties long done, this tower quietly stands guard over the farmstead which has grown up around it. A fortified house of vernacular character, it probably always has had a close association with farming and the land, and the cut-down remains of its immediate successor, a two-storeyed farmhouse of mid 18th-century date, stands next door. The tower is a plain, no-nonsense affair with few decorative frills, somehow embodying the virtues of probity and austerity inscribed in Latin on a panel above the door: 'Keep hidden what is secret; speak little; be truthful; avoid wine; remember death; be pitiful'. It is laid out on an L-plan. The projecting wing contains the stair, and incorporates a gun-loop ascribable to *c* 1570; inside, however, there are indications that this wing is an addition to an oblong tower of, perhaps, mid 16th-century date.

The walls are rounded at the angles, such a form being easier and cheaper to construct with small rubble and pinnings. Most of the window-openings were enlarged in the 18th century. The parapet has a plain straight cope and is projected on moulded corbels. A stair-passage to the open wall-walk is contained within a turret which spans the re-entrant angle.

The 16th-century interior was re-arranged and sub-divided in the 18th century. The main vaulted cellar on the ground floor has a kitchen fireplace whose surround was re-assembled from parts of the original hall fireplace. A slop-sink drains through the south wall. The first floor originally comprised one room, the laird's hall, heated by a large fireplace in the east end wall; smaller fireplaces were formed to match the smaller sub-divisions. The complex arrangement of openings and passages around the entrances to the first and second floors hints at an earlier layout before the addition of the stair wing. The second floor was originally sub-divided into two main (bed) chambers, each with a fireplace and a latrine; the external base of the latrine vent can be seen in the centre of the south wall at ground level.

The lands of Drumcoltran lay within the lordship of Kirkgunzeon, the superiority of which in 1550 passed from the Lords Herries to the Lords Maxwell. The lairds of Drumcoltran were a minor family of the same name, and the probable builder of the tower around 1570 was Edward Maxwell (d. 1609), second son of Edward Maxwell of Hills. The mortgaged lands of Drumcoltran passed to the Irving family in 1668 and remained in their possession until 1799. They were no doubt responsible for most of the alterations to the tower and the construction of the later house.

32* Carsluith Castle

16th century AD.

NX 494541. Signposted and clearly seen from the A 75 about 1 km SE of Carsluith village.

Historic Scotland.

Like Drumcoltran (no. 31), this well-preserved four-storeyed tower presides over a later farm court. Also like Drumcoltran, its later wing demonstrates a trend in contemporary house design. Originally, this was a simple oblong tower of early 16th-century date, and the upper floors were reached from a narrow stair contained in the north-west angle. The existing stair-turret was added in 1568, the date and the armorial of the Brown family being carved on a panel above the entrance-doorway. A few corbels are all that remain of the early parapet on the north side-wall, although rather more of the original upperworks survive on the end walls. The gun-ports disposed around the ground floor of the main block were probably also inserted in about 1568.

Inside, the effects of the addition can be detected in the arrangement of intra-mural passages and chambers between the stair and main block. The tower otherwise conforms to the normal pattern: vaulted ground-floor cellarage, first-floor hall, second-floor chambers with attic and caphouse over the stair. In this case there are two ground-floor vaults but no inbuilt kitchen. Food was probably prepared in an outhouse or in the hall itself where there is a slop-sink in the south-west corner; for dry preservatives the hall fireplace has a salt-box in one jamb. The two (bed) chambers on the second floor are of mirrored layout, the partition having formerly run between the paired latrines in the south wall.

Little is known of its history. Carsluith was Church land in the Middle Ages, and held until 1748 by the Browns, a family of Cumbrian origin. In 1579 a member of the family of John Brown, builder of the addition, probably his son, was implicated in the murder of his neighbour, John McCulloch of Barholm.

33 Dunskey Castle

16th century AD.

NX 003533. Reached from cliff-top footpath which ascends from the old quarry at the S end of Portpatrick waterfront.

Perched on a sea cliff, the ruins of this castle occupy the most spectacular coastal setting of any in south-west Scotland. It is a substantial ruin too, presenting a 30.2 m-long landward front on the edge of a 15 m-wide rock-cut ditch. Entry is through an arched gateway in this wall which was originally secured with a sliding drawbar. The promontory on which the castle stands is enclosed within the remains of a circuit-wall; vestiges of a watch-tower lie at the seaward extremity, and foundations of a building, probably including a kitchen, adjoin the south angle of the tower.

Carsluith Castle
(Left)

Dunskey Castle: engraving, 1789

Dunskey Castle

**Orchardton
Castle: laver**
(Right)

The ditch and parts of the enclosure may have formed part of an earlier castle of the Adair family; a castle has been on record since the 14th century, but some time before 1503 it was invested and burnt by the fearsome McCullochs of Myrton and Cardoness. The nucleus of the tower was built early in the 16th century by William Adair of Kinhilt (d. 1513), probable builder also of Stranraer Castle (no. 15). It was later added to and remodelled, the most likely patron for this work being Viscount Montgomery, laird of Dunskey from 1608 until his death in 1636. After his acquisition of the estate in 1648 the Reverend James Blair moved to Killantringan, and already by 1684 this castle was 'wholly ruinous'.

The main block is a sizeable L-plan tower with a later long gallery range to the north-west. The arrangement of rooms follows the usual pattern: vaulted cellars on the ground floor, main public rooms on the first floor, and private chambers on the upper floors. On the first floor, the great hall takes up the whole of the main block, and leads through to the gallery. On the ground floor, the layout around the entrance has been complicated by the later insertion of a large scale-and-platt (straight-flighted) staircase. Previously, the main stair ascended the turret in the re-entrant angle, while the wing may have contained the original kitchen before it was out-housed. Curiously, the water-supply, a well-chamber beneath the east wall, appears to have been accessible only from the outside. The northernmost cellar in the main building was designed for access only from the courtyard, not from within, possibly for stabling. Two dark unlit chambers on the ground floor suggest a more sinister purpose; every good castle should have at least one really unpleasant prison-cell!

34* Orchardton Castle

15th century AD.

NX 817551. Signposted on the A 711 S of Palnackie.

Historic Scotland.

Orchardton is the only known cylindrical tower-house in Scotland, but why it should enjoy this unique status is not clear. There are at least 23 buildings of this class in Ireland, so the builder or mason might be suspected of having an Irish ancestry. However, although Galloway as a whole is an area of presumptive Irish influence, proof of any special links with Orchardton has not yet been found.

The lands of Orchardton, formerly known as Glenshinnoch, were in the possession of the Cairns family from the early 15th century until 1633 when they passed, through an heiress, to the Maxwell family of Drumcoltran (no. 31). The date of the building of the tower is not recorded, but it can be ascribed to the latter half, possibly the last quarter, of the 15th century. In terms of defence, there appears to be nothing specially advantageous about its position in rolling farmland.

The circular tower was never alone. An adjacent range to the south-west, although reduced to ruins, provided much storage space in its ground-floor vaults, and would have had a sizeable hall and chambers above. Intercommunication between this range and the tower was through what is now a window on the south side. This original first-floor entry to the tower was probably associated with a wooden staircase; the existing first-floor doorway has been converted from a window, and is approached by a stone forestair. The vaulted ground-floor cellar of the tower has separate access through an arch-pointed doorway. The rubble walls are crowned by a corbelled parapet, some of the moulded corbels bearing carved faces.

Walls of 1.8 m thickness do not create a spacious interior: each room on the three upper floors is merely 5.2 m in diameter. Cosiness and clutter, not commodiousness, must have been the order of the day. The rooms were heated and their larger windows fitted with bench-seats in the ingoings. Although no different in size, the first-floor 'hall' has a couple of superior details: near the fireplace there is a decorative laver for rinsing hands and vessels; on the opposite wall, close to the foot of the stair, there is a moulded stone lamp-bracket. The newel (spiral) stair is formed within the wall thickness, as are the small dry closets on each floor. At the head of the stair, the open parapet wall-walk has stepped slabs and drainage-runnels.

The top of the tower also commands pleasing views over the surrounding countryside. But as one gazes, one wonders: why was the tower placed just here, and why is it cylindrical? Orchardton is a delightful enigma.

35 Lochwood Castle

15th century AD and later.

NY 084968. On the W side of a minor road linking the A 701 and B 7020 over 5 km S of Beattock.

Standing in ancient woodland on the edge of Lochwood Moss this castle was the fortified residence of the Johnstone family in Annandale from the 12th to the early 18th century. At the northern end of the site is a motte with an unusual terraced profile; this was

the family's first home, probably a timber-built tower associated with a palisaded enclosure. This structure was superseded by a larger stone-built castle, the main element of which was an L-plan tower of late 15th-century date, possibly incorporating earlier fragments in re-use. The tower now survives only to first-floor level above vaulted cellars and a prison. A recent programme of clearance and consolidation has also revealed extensive ranges of buildings within the courtyard.

Lochwood was captured and occupied by the English from 1547 to 1550. They described it as 'a fair large tower, able to lodge all our company safely, with a barmkin, hall, kitchen and stables, all within the barmkin ...'. In 1585 the castle was attacked and burnt by the Maxwells, jealous of the rising power of the Johnstones, but life at Lochwood became more peaceful in the 17th century. In the fields to the south and west of the ruins are traces of a garden which had a circular mound as its centrepiece, testimony, perhaps, to more settled conditions during the last phase of occupation.

36* Cardoness Castle

15th century AD.

NX 590552. Situated on the roadside (A 75) about 1 km SW of Gatehouse of Fleet; signposted.

Historic Scotland.

From its rocky ridge overlooking the Water of Fleet, Cardoness Castle presents a plain but commanding face to the world. Inside, it contains all the accommodation and amenities that a medieval laird could desire. The tower was built in the last decades of the 15th century, probably by Alexander McCulloch, a close associate of King James IV. The McCulloch family of Myrton and Cardoness were seemingly as tough as their castle and not quite so passive! The tower was their residence until 1622 when the mortgaged estate was acquired by the Gordons of Upper Ardwall, but later members of the family violently refused to accept the change of ownership. At their hands in 1668 the sick widow of a Gordon laird was dragged outside to die, and in 1697 a member of the same family was shot and fatally wounded. The tower has been uninhabited since the end of the 17th century.

Lochwood Castle
(Left)

Cardoness Castle by William Daniell, 1814

Cardoness Castle: 'inverted keyhole' gun port

The position of the castle was described by an English spy in *c* 1563-6. At that time, long before the Fleet was canalised, it was reckoned to be a riverside strength of some military potential: 'at the full sea, boats of eight tons may come under the wall. It ... may be kept with one hundred men in garrison', but it was 'without a barmkin, and without battaling [battlements]'. Where it drew its water-supply has not been ascertained.

For close-range defence the tower relied on its thick walls and gun-ports of 'inverted keyhole' type for use with hand-held firearms. The entrance, placed trustingly at ground-level, had a stout wooden door and draw-bar, further protected with an inner wrought-iron yett (gate). A hatch in the ceiling of the entrance-passage is similar to the Irish feature known expressively as a 'murder hole'; no doubt it also served

a peaceable function for raising and lowering goods and equipment.

As usual, the lowest floor was set aside for storage and services, with living quarters on the upper floors. The ground floor of this tower originally comprised two cellars, and an intermediate wooden floor for storage was formed within the vault. The larger cellar has two circular recesses for water or pickling-tubs, and a slop-sink for discharging liquid waste matter. A pit-prison is set within the east end wall, reached through a hatch in the floor above. Access to the upper floors is obtained by a newel stair in the south-east angle. The first floor is taken up with the hall, the principal room in the castle. The second floor contained two private chambers, including the master bedroom, and there were lesser chambers on the third floor and in the attic.

In its domestic fixtures Cardoness is a model of what all the best towers possessed in about 1500. There was a generous provision of latrines with intra-mural vents, at least one on each floor. All the main living-rooms were heated, and the principal fireplaces have fashionable moulded surrounds. The decorative cupboard near the hall fireplace was probably for the display of plate and valuables. The embrasures of the larger window-openings have stone bench-seats, and the openings themselves were half-shuttered, half-glazed. Sitting at the windows enjoying the air and the views, McCulloch ladies must surely have added a measure of grace and good temper to the domestic scene.

37* Comlongon Castle

c 1500 AD.

NY 079689. The approach track, signposted, is on the W side of the B 724 at the N end of Clarencefield village.

Now partly shrouded in trees, the massive bulk of this exceptionally complete tower once dominated the surrounding flat landscape. It still conveys an impression of grim solidity, its red sandstone masonry adorned only by a corbelled parapet with Irish-style roofed turrets. The overall martial effect, however, is tempered by the adjacent mansion whose presence shows that there has always been more to this position than mere defence. Internally, a roofed tower such as this admirably recreates the setting and atmosphere of home life among the late medieval nobility.

Comlongon Castle

It was built, probably in about 1500, by the Murrays of Cockpool, who were descended from Thomas Randolph, Earl of Moray and Lord of Nithsdale. Nothing now remains of their earliest residence in this vicinity; this tower formed part of the barony of Cockpool when it was created in 1508, and remained until recently in the possession of the Murrays' descendants, the Earls of Mansfield.

The walls of Comlongon are particularly thick. The north wall, in which the entrance (with its wrought-iron gate or yett) is placed, is 4.1 m in thickness, and is honeycombed with vaulted mural chambers. Some served as bed closets opening off the main rooms; one chamber, entered from the first-floor hall, served a more sinister purpose as guard-room for prison-cells beyond and beneath. The pit-prison is a frightful unlit hole reached through a hatch in the floor of the ante-chamber.

The layout follows, with variations, a standard late medieval pattern: on the ground floor a vaulted cellar incorporating a well, a circular barrel-recess and a wooden-floored entresol for extra storage; a first-floor hall-kitchen (an especially noteworthy feature), hall and kitchen fireplaces being at opposite ends of the room, doubtless separated by wooden screens; and paired chambers on the second and third floors, all provided with fireplaces, windows with stone bench-seats, and latrines. At parapet level there are roofed turrets and a long gallery of late 16th-century date.

The focus of chivalric pride was the hall fireplace. It is associated with an ornate aumbry or cupboard in the south wall, which has a cusped head formed unevenly in two pieces. The fireplace is spanned by a wooden lintel, and has moulded jambs and a carved cornice. It is structurally protected by a relieving-arch above, the gap between the arch and the cornice being originally infilled with clay for heat resistance and flexibility. High on the chimney-breast is a panel bearing a version of the royal arms, flanked by corbels displaying Murray armorials. There are other heraldic corbels in the side-walls, some fairly indistinct.

Comlongon Castle: hall fireplace and aumbry by Thomas Ross

38* Threave Castle

14th century AD and later.

NX 739622. Situated on an island in the River Dee. Car park is at Kelton Mains Farm, and a footpath, 0.8 km long, leads to the jetty from which a small boat ferries visitors to the island. Signposted on the A 75 W of Castle Douglas.

Historic Scotland and NTS.

Stark and uncompromising in a flat and watery landscape, Threave Castle is a menacing giant of a tower. Set with an aura of gloomy majesty on its island fastness, this building still receives the awe and respect that its medieval owners intended. Appropriately, it was the main power base of the Black Douglases, who were for about a century before their forfeiture in 1455 the most powerful of the Scottish nobility and a constant thorn in the side of the early Stewart kings. The island may have been an early centre of Galloway lordship, and the tower was built after the acquisition of that lordship in 1369 by Archibald, 3rd Earl of Douglas. Unfortunately, the actions and ambitions of the later earls collided with those of King James II, and a sustained royal campaign against the Douglases in the early 1450s culminated in sieges of their major strongholds in 1455, including a two-month siege of Threave.

From 1455 custody of the castle and the office of Steward of Kirkcudbright were vested in a succession of royal appointees, and from 1526 were heritably attached to the Lords Maxwell. The castle was briefly in English possession in 1545, and in 1588 the suspect loyalty of the Catholic Maxwells brought a royal army to the region. But the castle and its keeper honourably discharged their final duty in defence of the reigning monarch when, in 1640, Robert Maxwell, 1st Earl of Nithsdale, and his garrison resisted a 13-week siege by a Covenanting army, surrendering only upon the king's order. Later that year the local War Committee decided that the castle be partly dismantled to make it unusable. Apart from minor modifications made during the Napoleonic Wars, that is how the castle remained until taken into State custody in 1913.

Since 1913 the castle has been scrupulously preserved, and some of its less obvious qualities (and many exciting artefacts) have been brought to light by archaeological excavations. Thanks to such efforts, Threave now boasts the most complete medieval riverside harbour discovered in Scotland. It would have admitted small boats of shallow draught, required especially when the river ford at the southern end of the island was impassable. The harbour-walls were of timber and stone construction, and because of its water-girt position the tower itself is probably laid on a timber raft foundation.

Threave Castle: building of artillery work; re-construction by GD Hay

wall-head, 26 m above the ground, is part of a slotted platform from which offensive objects could be dropped on unwanted visitors. Around the head of the tower on the other three sides are three rows of sockets which originally held the cantilevered timbers of a framed wooden gallery, a suggested reconstruction being depicted in the accompanying drawing.

Inside, the entrance opens on to an intermediate level ceiled with a stone barrel vault. The south end of this entresol was the kitchen, and the basement, formerly reached by ladder, contained the well, storage cellars, and a prison. The newel stair is the key to the layout of any tower; here it is set within the west angle. The great hall takes up the second floor, and is provided with a grand fireplace and large mullioned and transomed windows set within stone-benched embrasures; the latrines on all floors are in the south angle. There are paired chambers on the floor above, and slots in the walls indicate strutted timberwork used in the construction of the floors. The topmost floor was unheated, and had no less than nine windows together with a doorway that led out on to the wall-head platform, no doubt a busy place in time of siege.

Threave Castle: aerial view (Left)

Befitting the pre-eminence of its owners, this is the earliest and largest tower in the region, probably archetypal to many Galloway lairds and their masons, whether they regarded the Douglases with affection, envy or fear. The original entry was later lowered and narrowed to its present position and width, but was still reached by a timber stair. Directly above, at the

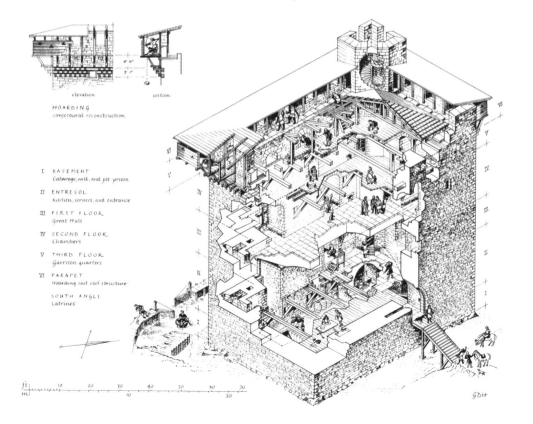

elevation   section

HOARDING
conjectural reconstruction

I BASEMENT
Cellarage, well, and pit-prison

II ENTRESOL
Kitchen, services, and entrance

III FIRST FLOOR
Great Hall

IV SECOND FLOOR
Chambers

V THIRD FLOOR
Garrison quarters

VI PARAPET
Hoarding and roof structure

SOUTH ANGLE
Latrines

Threave Castle: cut-out isometric reconstruction by GD Hay

Ancillary buildings provided the extra services and accommodation needed to sustain the noble household. A low earthen bank may represent the circuit of an early apron-like enclosure, but the tower acquired a more regular and closely-fitting curtain-wall. Two straight stretches of this wall survive, fronted by a ditch and incorporating a gateway which shows the impress of a drawbridge in an uplifted position. The loopholed walls have a sloping outer face and projecting circular angle-turrets equipped with gun-ports. There are grounds for doubting the claim that this was the work of the 8th Earl of Douglas in about 1450, anticipating trouble from James II, and ascribing it instead to the subsequent period of royal custody.

Morton Castle

39 Morton Castle

14th century AD.

NX 890992. In gated field on S shore of Morton Loch; best approached by unclassified road from A 702 at NX 874999.

Historic Scotland.

Set against the Lowther Hills, Morton Castle is as remote and imperfectly understood as any castle can be. Its position, purpose, style, and its date are all open to question, yet it is one of those rare buildings that still manages to convey the mystical aura of the Age of Chivalry. Only the central core of the castle survives upstanding: a two-storeyed hall block attached to part of a turreted gatehouse at the west end, and to a segment of a substantial angle-tower at the other. Throughout, the walls are faced with ashlar masonry, a silver-grey sandstone of local extraction. In the gatehouse area, only half of the passage and one of the flanking D-shaped towers remains standing; the

position of the drawbridge is reduced to footings. We can see in the side wall the slot for the portcullis, and the corbels which show that the passage was timber-ceiled, not vaulted. The basement of the adjacent tower contained a prison which was lit and ventilated only by a small aperture.

The hall is now entered by a later doorway from the gatehouse passage. Originally, it was reached via a stair-turret and through the arch-pointed doorway at the western end of the rear (north) wall. The first floor has been a long and grand room, divided up with screens and lit by large mullioned and transomed windows; vestiges of the canopied fireplace can be seen in the south side-wall. On the ground floor, which probably served as a kitchen-cum-lower hall, there is another canopied fireplace in the east end-wall. It was lit by a series of small oblong windows, one of which is associated with a slop-sink. Private chambers were contained in the south-eastern tower, with a latrines-system in which vertical vents discharged into a lower sloping drain. The (?pit-prison) basement of this tower was vaulted, the only surviving indication of vaulting within the castle.

Within the hall there are the foundations and roof-outlines of two-storeyed buildings inserted and occupied in the 17th and 18th centuries. The tile-demarcated areas represent work of repair carried out in modern times. Footings of cottages which are known to have stood outside the gatehouse in the 18th century are also visible. Original ancillary structures stood against the north wall of the hall, and, like the rest of the castle, incorporated much timberwork, presumably from Nithsdale's oak woods.

Given the availability of the whole promontory, the castle seems to be tightly restricted to an area which has put the ends of the building at structural risk. This position has few defensive advantages, and in height the castle would have merely corresponded with the crest of the nearby hill. The loch and the dam-wall are comparatively modern, perhaps taking the place of marshland around the burn. On the landward side, the approach-track spans a great ditch, and along the inner edge of this ditch there are traces of curtain-walls, building-stances, and artificial scarping. Some of these elements of fortification may ante-date the upstanding castle, which has been ascribed to various dates between the later 13th and the mid 15th centuries.

The lordship of Morton comes on record in the 1170s in possession of Hugh Sansmanche (*sine manicis*, sleeveless), possibly acquired through marriage to a daughter of Ralph, son of Dunegal, native lord of Nithsdale. The lands passed to Thomas Randolph, although 'le manoir de Morton' was temporarily forfeited to the English after 1306, and Morton was one of the Nithsdale castles allegedly demolished in 1356-7. In 1369/70 the conveyance of the lands by Thomas Randolph's successor to James Douglas received royal confirmation. The upstanding structure almost certainly belongs to the Douglas period of ownership, probably serving as a country retreat or hunting lodge; it was in existence in 1440 when the barony was granted to James Douglas, Lord of Dalkeith, and (from 1458) Earl of Morton. Although briefly in the hands of the Lords Maxwell in the 1580s, ownership otherwise remained with the Douglases.

40 Kirkcudbright, Castledykes

13th/14th centuries AD.

NX 677508. Reached by footpath, Castledykes Walk, from W side of (N) High Street, or through the grounds of the Academy.

What was once a royal castle now survives as enigmatic humps and hollows in a flat riverside field a short distance downstream from Kirkcudbright. On closer examination these remains reveal themselves to be the foundations of a stone-built stronghold of some magnitude. Excavation in 1911-13 showed that within a surrounding ditch, originally a wet moat,

were the walls of a courtyard castle with a double-towered gatehouse facing north-east. Unusually, the gatehouse towers were buttressed. The curtain walls had had rounded towers at the angles, including a larger donjon at the south-west. The finds were particularly rich in pottery and ironwork, including eight imported French jugs (Stewartry Museum).

The castle first appears on record in 1288, held by one of the four Guardians of the realm. Although the layout is reminiscent of an 'Edwardian' castle, there is no evidence that Edward I of England had a direct hand in its construction. However, he did stay here for a few days in July 1300, and it appears as an English supply-base until 1306-7. Little is known of its history during Douglas ownership. It may have served as a refuge for Henry VI of England after the Battle of Towton in 1461, and was probably last used as a residence by James IV on journeys to and from Whithorn. In 1509 possession of the castle lands passed to the burgh.

41* Caerlaverock Castle

c AD 1300 and later.

NY 025656. Signposted from the B 725, 14 km SE of Dumfries.

Historic Scotland.

Caerlaverock is, without doubt, the region's premier castle. Its appearance in dazzling red sandstone conveys an impression both of solid strength and dignified splendour. The double-towered gatehouse

Caerlaverock Castle: by David Roberts c1850

Caerlaverock Castle

Aerial view
(Top right)

Caerlaverock Castle: Nithsdale's Building

and triangular layout, surrounded by a water-filled moat and earthen rampart, display some of the changes in design that were induced partly by Edward I's castle-building activities in the last quarter of the 13th century. Caerlaverock itself is of late 13th-century origin, its builder, Sir Herbert de Maxwell, being a nephew of the first Maxwell owner of the lands of Caerlaverock.

By 1300 the castle housed a Scots garrison which harassed English-held Lochmaben (no. 42). Accordingly, in that year, Edward I went out of his way to take Caerlaverock, a siege operation recorded by the author of a contemporary Anglo-Norman ballad. To him, 'Caerlaverock was so strong a castle that it feared no siege before the King came there ... In shape it was like a shield, for it had but three sides round it, with a tower at each corner, but one of them was a double one, so high, so long, and so wide, that the gate was underneath it, well made and strong, with a drawbridge and a sufficiency of other defences. And it had good walls, and good ditches filled right up to the brim with water ...'

The singular shape of the castle is recognisable in this description. Much of the original masonry is still discernible, particularly in the western curtain-wall and gatehouse-tower, although Caerlaverock suffered badly in the course of later Anglo-Scottish warfare. But just how far the 'destructions' wrought in about 1312 (by the Scots) and 1356-7 (by the English) rendered the castle unusable, and how much rebuilding was undertaken in the 14th century are difficult questions to answer. It is clear that the defences of the castle were restored and improved in

the 15th and 16th centuries by the Lords Maxwell, whose armorial is carved above the main gateway. The curtain-walls and eastern gatehouse-tower were reconstructed, and additions were made to the gatehouse itself; the wide-mouthed gun-ports were probably inserted when repairs were in hand in 1593. The castle was among those 'thrown down' by an English army in 1570, palpably an over-statement, whereas the effects of the final episode in the active use of the castle cannot be gainsaid. In 1640 a Royalist garrison under Robert Maxwell, 1st Lord Nithsdale, capitulated after a 13-week siege and bombardment by an army of the Estates, the castle thereafter being partly dismantled to prevent its further occupation.

The vigorous history of this frontier castle satisfyingly bears out its martial appearance, but it was a residence as well as a stronghold. Originally the main hall was on the first floor of the gatehouse block, but was later sub-divided. The 15th-century range on the western side of the courtyard contains a series of chambers, probably for guest accommodation. Little survives of the hall block built along the inside of the south curtain in the 1630s, although its doorway gives some idea of its former grandeur. The three-storeyed east range, Nithsdale's building (1634), had a symmetrical six-bay ashlar facade, of which four bays survive intact; the openings have moulded surrounds and carved pediments bearing armorials and relief sculptures. The service basement, which incorporates the castle well, is of early origin; the upper floors were served by a spacious staircase, and most rooms were well equipped with windows, latrines, and fireplaces.

The splendours of Caerlaverock divert attention from the peculiarity of its low-lying setting, close to the edge of woodland swamps and overlooked from the north. An English report of 1563-6 was sceptical of its capabilities 'unless the hill above the same, called the Ward Law, be fortified ...'. However, it had some advantages insofar as 'boats ... of ten tons will come to the foot of this hill at the full sea'. Among the trees and swamps some 180 m to the south of the castle is one of the great unsolved mysteries of Caerlaverock: a large, oblong, and formerly moated platform which has revealed traces of medieval masonry (NX 027656).

It may have been a 'failed' 13th-century precursor of the existing castle; timber recovered from the site has pointed to a construction date of *c* 1225, a product perhaps of Sir John Maxwell, first Maxwell lord of Caerlaverock. Immediately after the fall of Caerlaverock in 1300, Edward I reconstructed the peel at Dumfries on a large scale, involving the import and trans-shipment of much Cumbrian timber; it is possible that this structure at Caerlaverock may also belong to the English period between 1300 and 1312.

42 Lochmaben Castles

12th—16th centuries AD.

NY 088811, 082822. Signposted from B 7020 and A 709 at the S end of Lochmaben. Check at golf clubhouse for access to motte.

Historic Scotland.

The earliest Bruce castle is a motte which now does service as the 14th tee on the golf-course south-west of the town. Its summit is unusually large and oval on plan, and is partly surrounded by a ditch. Artefacts recovered from the site are in Nithsdale District Museum, Dumfries.

It was superseded in the later 13th or 14th century by the stone castle which occupies a promontory at the southern end of Castle Loch, a stretch of water that

Lochmaben Castle: conjectural reconstruction

Lochmaben Castle

Bayeux Tapestry: motte-building
(Top right)

has always been renowned for its fish. Immediately to the south of the castle, an earthen platform marks the position of a moated and timber-palisaded enclosure (a peel) built by Edward I of England in 1298. Peel and stone castle were protected by outer ditches and ramparts.

The most remarkable feature of the stone castle is a 6.1 m wide canal which fronts the south curtain-wall. The canal is spanned by tall wing-walls which are arched, probably to accommodate boats when the level of the loch was higher. Some curtain-walls survive almost to their original heights, but are mainly reduced to rubble core; ashlar masonry can be seen around the edges of the canal. The counterweight pit for a drawbridge is clearly visible in the centre of the south wall. This gateway was backed by a passage running beneath what was possibly a gatehouse and great hall range, of which only the foundations now survive.

From 1298 until the Union of Crowns in 1603 Lochmaben was of vital strategic importance in the ebb and flow of Anglo-Scottish warfare. For much of the 14th century it was in English hands, and in 1373-6 extensive repairs and additions were made. It was eventually surrendered to the Scots under the Earl of Douglas in 1384 and became a royal castle, King James IV later residing here from time to time. During his reign a great hall was built, and the castle was later described as 'the king's own house and of the greatest strength of any in this west border of Scotland'. From 1524 until 1588 keepership was vested in the Lords Maxwell, but the castle suffered because of their feud with the Johnstones and their Catholic sympathies.

Although steps were taken to maintain the castle in 1624-5, its days as a garrisoned military stronghold had effectively passed in 1603.

43 Druchtag Motte

12th century AD.

NX 349466. On E roadside just N of Mochrum village; signposted.

Historic Scotland.

When they first come on record in the later Middle Ages, the lands of Druchtag formed part of the barony of Mochrum and were held by the McCullochs of Druchtag. Nothing is known, however, about the state of feudal lordship when this castle was thrown up, probably in the later 12th century. The village of Kirk of Mochrum, a short distance to the south, may have originated alongside it.

The motte is as typical as any structure of its kind can be: a steep-sided mound in the pudding-shaped mould, it lacks its timber defences and buildings but is otherwise straight out of the fabric of the Bayeux Tapestry. Except on the roadside bank, the base of the motte is encircled by a deep and wide ditch, the upcast of which formed the mound itself and the low outer rim known as a counterscarp bank. The summit area is level and roughly circular on plan, just over 20 m in diameter. There is no clear evidence of a bridged approach.

Druchtag Motte

44 Motte of Urr

12th century AD.

NX 815646. On the W side of the B 794 and the Urr Water, NNW of Dalbeattie; cross the river by footbridge and call at Milton of Buittle Farm before visit.

Covering an area of about 2 hectares, this truly impressive earthwork is the most extensive motte-and-bailey castle in Scotland. Only perhaps from the air can one appreciate its great size, looking for all the world like some great earthen battleship stranded on the alluvial river plain. Its position in the valley is not especially commanding; it may originally have been an island, but the river now flows in a single channel to the east. Close up, its deep outer ditch puts one in mind of an iron-age hillfort, and it is possible that the bailey was developed out of an existing fortification in Anglo-Norman times.

The lower slopes have been artificially scarped on the north and east. A 15 m-wide ditch surrounds the entire work, and is bridged by causeways in the south-eastern and north-western sectors. Low counterscarp banks can be seen around the lips of this ditch, and the enclosure thus formed is about 150 m in maximum length. The motte itself, set within its own ditch, occupies most of the southern end of the enclosure; it rises in the usual 'pudding' or truncated cone form to a sub-circular summit area. Archaeological excavation of part of the motte top showed that the upper 1.83 m had been added following the destruction by fire of 12th-century timber buildings and palisades; coins and pottery in the upper levels indicated that occupation had continued into the 14th century.

The earliest available records show the lordship of Urr in the possession of Walter de Berkeley (d. *c* 1194), chamberlain of William I. From him it passed by marriage to a cadet branch of the Balliols, the main line of that family later occupying nearby Buittle Castle. Two witnesses to a Balliol of Urr charter of 1262 were described as burgesses of Urr, but where this burgh settlement was located, whether inside or outside the bailey, and how long it lasted, are not known.

Motte of Urr: aerial view

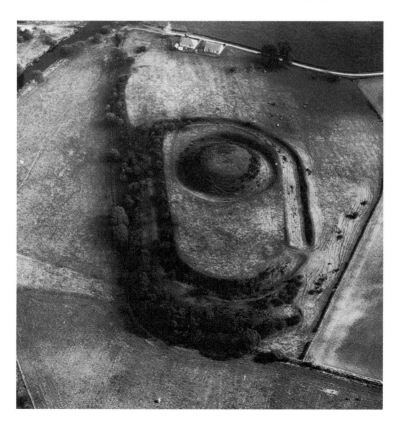

EARLY FORTIFICATIONS AND SETTLEMENTS

Castle O'er Fort:
aerial view

The beginnings of feudalism in Dumfries and Galloway in the 12th century mark a new departure in the history of landownership and settlement in the region. But there were underlying elements inherited from earlier, pre-feudal times. By their names, centres of medieval lordship such as Buittle and Morton (no. 39) betray the ancient ancestry of their sites, whilst others, including possibly the Motte of Urr (no. 44), also appear to retain physical evidence. The habit of living or taking refuge on commanding hilltops such as Tynron Doon (no. 47) or on islands obviously died hard, and a proportion of prehistoric and post-Roman sites in this region show significant signs of medieval occupation.

Continuity in the actual principles and techniques of fortification is evident too. There was probably not much that feudal sappers could have taught their predecessors about the building of ramparts and ditches (including rock-cut ditches), or earth, timber and stone superstructures. The fact that we now see early fortifications in much reduced condition, either as low earthen mounds or heaps of stony debris, sometimes vitrified (that is, heat-fused), should not deceive us into underestimating the organisation, skill and tools which went into their construction.

Brochs, the structural masterpieces of prehistoric Scotland, display such qualities developed over several centuries after 500 BC. They are thick-walled circular towers of two or more storeys, built mainly but by no means always on the coast and of a defensive or at least a security-conscious disposition. Western Galloway can claim a few, albeit very humble specimens (no. 53) compared to those of northern and western Scotland.

The Romans too command automatic respect as masters of military strategy and of well-organised, well-built fortifications (nos 48-52). There is an uncanny resemblance between the Roman army and the English invading forces of Edward I (d. 1307), not least in the pattern of control that they sought to establish around the main western routes into Scotland, and possibly in their overland campaigns across Galloway. Edward reached and fought around the River Cree in 1300, and his son's army got as far as Whithorn and Loch Ryan in 1301. The Romans had maritime and cartographic knowledge of Loch Ryan, the *Rerigonius Sinus* and *Rerigonium* of Ptolemy's map, but physical proof of their presence in the west has not yet advanced beyond the fortlet at Gatehouse of Fleet (NX 595574, visible only as a cropmark from the air).

The distinctive qualities of Roman fortifications and the military logic which dictated their sequence make them admirable targets for aerial survey. In Nithsdale they have been tracked from the air as far north as a fortlet at Sanquhar (NX 775106), one of the more exciting recent discoveries being that of a fort visible as a parchmark in the policies of Drumlanrig Castle (no. 25) at NX 854989. Tibbers Castle (NX 862982), rebuilt by a client of Edward I, lies significantly close at hand; obviously great military minds thought alike.

Our knowledge of the native background in the Roman and post-Roman periods is sketchy. Galloway was inhabited by Britons who formed the tribe of the Novantae. Where their area of influence met, or overlapped with, those of the Selgovae and Brigantes east of the Nith and to which tribe the major hillfort of Burnswark (no. 52) belonged are not clear. By the 6th century the descendants of the tribes in this region were formed into the Celtic Christian kingdom of Rheged which was at its strongest in the period *c* 570-90. It was centred on the Eden valley, extending westwards presumably as far as Dunragit ('fort of Rheged'), although placenames suggest an Irish Gaelic infiltration in the Rhins by about this period.

By peaceful, or more likely by forceful, means, the Angles of Northumbria extended their control across Galloway in the course of the 7th century, there to remain as rulers for at least two centuries. Their imprint, however, was more in Christian sculpture than in secular building. Out of the confusion of Northumbrian collapse in the 9th and 10th centuries there emerged a Gaelic-Norse dynasty and populace made up of Scandinavian immigrants from north-west England and from Ireland, together with a special breed of Gaelic-speaking Irish incomers, the Gall Ghaidhill ('foreign Gael') after whom Galloway is named. In the 12th century Gallovidians were disparagingly described as 'Picts' by reason of their fierce and barbarous, not their racial qualities, there being no evidence of Pictish settlement in the south-west (cf no. 46). Of the forts and burial-places of these formidable warriors we know pitifully little, but Viking influence seems well attested in the Machars and around Kirkcudbright.

Despite this social and cultural maelstrom, 12th-century Galloway had become a distinct entity with its own laws and customs. How far it had acquired territorial definition is hard to say. The notion that a series of linear earthworks known as the 'Deil's Dyke' marked a northern frontier of the province in British or Anglian times, perhaps even by Strathclyde Britons against Anglian encroachment, is attractive, but unconvincing. The idea of a great march-dyke running from Loch Ryan to the Solway near Annan appears to have been the brain-child of the 19th-century antiquary, Joseph Train. Close examination of its supposed line in Galloway has shown that Train's Dyke has no existence in fact, being a disconnected series of tracks or local and late boundaries with no common structural character. A separate branch in upper Nithsdale runs north-westwards for some 27 km from NS 837049 and appears a more genuine and unitary earthwork with bank and ditch. However, excavation and research suggest a medieval origin for at least part of this work, possibly the boundary of a forest hunting reserve.

Boonies, enclosure and settlement

The pattern and character of prehistoric domestic settlement in the region is still a matter of active archaeological exploration. In the eastern uplands unenclosed homesteads and palisaded works containing timber-built round houses are beginning to come to light as, for example, on Gibb's Hill (NY 308841) and Potholm Hill (NY 362880). Such houses reveal themselves most often through excavation (eg nos 52, 55), but their stances are occasionally evident on the ground as they are within the hillfort of Castle O'er (no. 56). Compared to Romano-British settlement elsewhere in southern Scotland, the enclosed non-defensive homesteads of this area are noteworthy for their lack of stone-walled houses. These enclosures are characterised by the long use during the Roman period of timber or turf-and-timber round houses. Excavation within the oval- shaped and average-sized (0.07 ha) enclosure at Boonies (NY 304900) on a riverside terrace in Eskdale showed traces of up to 13 timber round houses representing a seven-phase sequence of building; for most of the time the homestead consisted of only one house and its yard, but in the final phase the interior was occupied by no less than five small houses. Quern-stones provided an indication of associated agricultural practices.

The nature of Romano-British settlement in Galloway remains imperfectly understood, although excavation of one of a pair of circular enclosures at Moss Raploch, Clatteringshaws (NX 554776), revealed a type of unenclosed stone-walled hut, tentatively ascribed to the 1st and 2nd centuries AD and akin to those of the Borders. In this instance, however, the building had external annexes and internal post-holes set close inside a wall of relatively slight thickness. Visitors to the Galloway Deer Museum at Clatteringshaws can inspect a reconstruction of this early circular dwelling erected just north of the visitor centre.

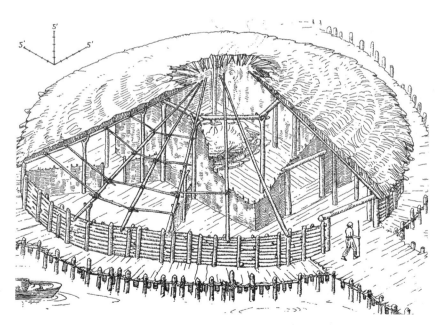

Milton Loch: reconstruction of crannog by Mrs CM Piggott

In Galloway the fullest information on the domestic aspects of iron-age settlement has come from the lacustrine version of the timber-built circular house, the crannog. These generally survive as stony artificial or 'improved' islands, most clearly visible in times of drought or when the surrounding waters have been drained. South-west Scotland is well known for its crannogs, and excavation of one in Milton Loch (NX 839718) produced clear evidence of the timber foundations, walls, causeway, and boat-dock associated with a 10.7 m diameter round house, occupied during the 2nd century AD and possibly earlier. Records of drainage operations in Carlingwark Loch (NX 765615) and Dowalton Loch (NX 4047), for example, describe the discovery of structures and relics of comparable date. The most conspicuous remains, however, are generally on islands occupied by medieval rectangular buildings (eg NX 762845, NX 903690, NX 898730, NX 293541). Walkers on the Southern Upland Way pass close to such structures in Loch Ochiltree (NX 3174), where there are crannogs of different types, and Loch Maberry (NX 285751).

Archaeologists are still learning to recognise possible hut-circles of bronze-age times, and the earliest farming communities of Dumfries and Galloway, those of the neolithic period, are as yet known to us through their burials rather than through their houses and agricultural activities. Their predecessors, the hunting-gathering-fishing communities of the mesolithic period, are elusive creatures detectable through their collections of flint implements, found mainly but not exclusively on the coast. Significant deposits have been located around the shores of Luce Bay, and mesolithic camp-sites have been identified at Low Clone (NX 334450) and Barsalloch (NX 343422). They occur on the edges of raised beaches, close to freshwater streams, and the site at Low Clone made use of a large scooped hollow; stake-holes and stone settings imply the construction of light shelters or sheds. A layer of carbonised wood from the hearth at Barsalloch was dated by radiocarbon analysis to around 4800 BC, making this the oldest dated settlement in Galloway, its occupants busily engaged with their flint industry at a time when post-glacial seas were at their greatest level.

Tynron Doon:
aerial view

45 Mote of Mark

5th century AD and later.

NX 845540. About 7 km SSE of Dalbeattie on the A 710, take the minor road to Rockcliffe, whence a signposted footpath, 0.5 km long, leads to the summit of the hill from the waterfront; the walk from Kippford is slightly longer.

NTS.

Occupying the summit of a low hill above the Urr estuary, this fort takes its name from Mark, King of Dumnonia, third party in the tragic romance of Tristan and Isolda. The association is a matter of legend, not of history, although interpretation of the archaeological excavations in 1913 and 1973 has shown that the site was occupied in the 5th and 6th centuries AD, broadly contemporary with the historical Tristan, and that the structure and artefacts were indeed of princely character. It was a citadel of some importance which lay within the British kingdom of Rheged and was destroyed in the 7th century, perhaps by Northumbrian Angles.

The hill is steep-sided and craggy to seaward, but more gently sloping on the landward side. The summit is undulating and consists of a pair of flat-topped rocky eminences with a natural soil-filled hollow in the middle. Around the edge there are the remains of a wall, now a low bank of stony debris incorporating pieces of heat-fused granite but originally a massive rampart of timber-laced drystone construction about 3 m high and 3 m thick. It had two entrances (on the south and north-western sides), and the central hollow, evidently the main area of occupation, had its own protective wall. The main rampart was fired by attackers, presumed Anglian, in the early 7th century who caused the stonework to become vitrified. The defences were later shored up with rubble, but these were soon dismantled and the site subjected to a final phase of squatter settlement.

The picture presented by the assemblage of artefacts is of a community which included metalworkers and jewellery-makers using crucibles and clay moulds for casting bronze objects. Among their products were brooches decorated with early forms of Celtic interlace; scraps of decorated glass, possibly from the Rhineland, were also used for inlays and enamels. Glass beads, jet objects, and quantities of pottery from the Bordeaux region were also among the finds which are now in the NMS. Here indeed is rich testimony to the life-style of the chieftains or princes of this fortified court, and to the workshops and craftsmen who served them.

46 Trusty's Hill, Anwoth, Fort and Symbol Stone

!st and 6th-7th centuries AD.

NX 588560. A footpath through the Boreland Hills from the W end of Gatehouse to Anwoth Church follows a straight course just to the N of this hill.

The fort on Trusty's Hill is one place in Galloway where the Picts are known to have left a recognisable mark. Carved on a rock beside the entrance passage are a series of Pictish symbols, including a water beast and a double disc traversed by a Z-shaped rod. Why these symbols are here, so far from Pictland, is a matter of speculation, but like other outliers in Mid Argyll they may commemorate the activities of a Pictish raiding party.

The burning of the fort as the result of such a raid may have been the cause of the vitrification evident in the remains of the stone rampart around the hilltop. This rampart, about 1.2 m thick and originally timber-laced, encloses a roughly oval summit area some 24 m by 15 m in extent with an entrance on the south side. On the north-eastern side a substantial bank and rock-cut ditch cuts through the neck of the promontory. Excavations in 1960 suggested that these defences belonged to the earliest phase of occupation, perhaps a fortified homestead of the Roman iron age; a small sub-circular stone-built hut of this period was located in the hollow on the east side of the entrance passage, opposite the symbol-carved rock. A later phase is represented by the outworks on natural rock shelves in front of the entrance, but these ramparts were of relatively slight construction, revetted only on their outer faces. The re-fortification belongs to a post-Roman period of military engineering, but whether a product of the Britons of Rheged or the Angles of Northumbria is hard to say.

The name itself, 'Trusty's Hill', probably has some association with this secondary phase, but the personal name from which it derives is as likely to have been a Celtic Tristan, matching Mark (no. 45), as a royal Pictish Drust. Legend and folklore refer to a Pictish king of this name who 'reigned' in Galloway in 523-8, but there is no evidence of Pictish settlement in the province. The name of the hill, like the symbol stone, may simply commemorate the signal military and logistical achievement of the leader of a Pictish task force!

47 Tynron Doon, Fort

1st millennium BC-16th century AD.

NX 819939. The hill stands above the northern road from the A 702 to Tynron village; the broad col to the W or the summit can be reached either from the S or from the NE, perhaps circling the hilltop round from Clonrae Farm.

'A very conspicuous object in the landscape for miles around ... and 'the most important fortress ... in the county' is how the qualities of this iron-age hillfort were summarised in the official Inventory of monuments in Dumfriesshire. It occupies the summit of a steep-sided spur of Auchengibbert Hill and stands to a height of 289 m OD. Its superb natural defences attracted further use of the site down to early modern times.

The summit plateau is sub-oval on plan, measuring about 45 m by 40 m, and is surrounded by a boulder-stone wall. A hut circle, 4.6 m in diameter, lies immediately to the east of the entrance, which is in the southern sector, and the interior contains other circular house stances. An L-plan tower-house, built before the last decade of the 16th century, stood at the north-western corner, and a stretch of lime-mortared walling along the south-eastern side, reported in 1920, was probably a fragment of its enclosure-wall.

A natural terrace on the north-eastern side below the summit has been bounded by a stony parapet, but man-made defences are otherwise confined to the western and south-western slopes. Very impressive they are too, comprising a stepped series of boldly scarped ramparts of earth and splintered rock gathered up from the intervening hollows. The lowest ditch or trench is rock-cut for most of its length.

The small finds recovered from the site and the surrounding slopes have a wide date-range. They include a significant proportion of material attributed to the Early Historic or 'Dark Age' period. Prominent among these was a portion of a gold filigree panel of a bracteate pendant of 6th-8th-century date Dumfries Museum.

48 Birrens, Roman Fort

1st and 2nd centuries AD.

NY 219751. SE of Lockerbie, in pasture immediately W of the Middlebie-Kirtlebridge road and N of the Mein Water.

Birrens was the first Roman fort in Scotland to be extensively excavated (in 1895), and, excavated again in 1936-7 and 1962-7, it has proved itself the most informative of all Roman sites in south-west Scotland. It is the only major fort in the region where there are unmistakeable, if slight, visible, remains, and it is the only one known to us by its original name, Blatobulgium. Its inclusion in the Antonine Itinerary (a Roman road map), where it is named, reflected its function as an outpost fort of Hadrian's Wall, 14 Roman miles on from Netherby (Castra Exploratorum) in Cumbria. The road through Birrens was the main western route into Scotland.

What one sees today is most of the central platform of the fort eroded at the south end by the Mein Water. The rampart is visible as a low mound, but most eye-catching are the corrugations of the six outer ditches at the north end traversed by a central causeway. Visible from the air, but not on the ground, are three temporary camps to the south and east of the fort, a large annexe to the west and, to the north, a large building interpreted as an inn.

Excavation and research have given us an almost complete picture of the building sequence and layout. Laid on the site of a late 1st-century fortlet, the Hadrianic fort of the 120s covered an area of 1.65 ha, had a turf rampart, timber buildings, and a large western annexe. In about AD 142, it was rebuilt and enlarged to 2.1 ha in order to accommodate a 1,000-strong garrison of the 1st

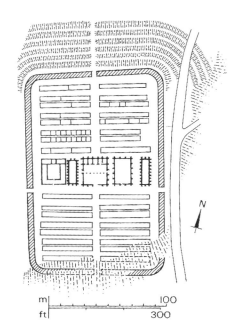

Birrens Roman Fort: plan showing results of excavation
(Far left)

Cohort Nervana Germanorum, a mixed unit of cavalry and infantry of the auxiliary army. This fort was characterised by the use of stone, which formed the bases of turf ramparts and provided dressed foundations for stone and perhaps stone-and-timber buildings. The barrack blocks were ranged on each side of a central group of administrative units, and consisted of narrow, closely-spaced pairs of buildings instead of the more usual wider ranges. This fort was destroyed and then rebuilt in AD 158 along similar lines. The new garrison consisted of the 2nd Cohort of Tungrians, likewise milliaria equitata. From *c* 163 for about 20 years it played an isolated role as an outpost of Hadrian's Wall, but it was finally abandoned by about AD 184, presumably as part of a reorganisation of troops in frontier posts.

Finds from the various excavations are in NMS, the Hunterian Museum, University of Glasgow, and Dumfries Museum. Over twenty inscribed stones, most now in Edinburgh, have been recovered from the site. These include a dedicatory tablet erected by the Tungrians in honour of their Emperor in AD 158. Three of the surviving altars refer to the two known milliary cohorts, whilst other inscribed fragments testify to the presence of the Sixth legion (Victorious).

49 Glenlochar, Roman Fort

1st and 2nd centuries AD.

NX 735645. NW of Castle Douglas, mainly in the field S or the B 795 and E of the River Dee.

Viewed from the road, which slices its north-western corner, this large fort of 3.3 ha shows up only slightly as a ditched platform. Viewed from the air, which is how it was first identified in 1949 (having previously been marked on maps as the supposed site of an abbey), it presents a detailed cropmark of characteristic gridded 'playing card' shape, complete with annexes and at least six temporary camps in the vicinity. Placed on the east bank of the River Dee, this was obviously a major centre of Roman control in Galloway, the westward limits of which are still unknown beyond Gatehouse (NX 595574).

Study of its layout as revealed by aerial photography has suggested comparison with Birrens (no. 48), and during the Antonine periods it could have housed a similar general purpose garrison, namely, a part-mounted milliary unit of the auxiliary army. The defences are especially

**Glenlochar
Roman Fort:
aerial view**

broad. Excavations in 1952 demonstrated a succession of three forts, preceded by an early and temporary Flavian occupation. The first, late Flavian (late 1st century), fort may have occupied part of the plateau closer to Glenlochar House, and ended in what was described as 'wholesale conflagration'; it was replaced by a fort of the first Antonine period, later modified.

50 Raeburnfoot, Roman Fort

1st century AD.

NY 251990. From the B 709, NW of Langholm, take the track to the farmhouse on the opposite (E) bank of the White Esk; the fort lies 90 m to the SW.

This small fort stands on a plateau just above the confluence of the River Esk and Rae Burn at Eskdalemuir, close to the point where the Roman road to Newstead can be assumed to have crossed the Esk and its flood plain. Raeburnfoot was probably a roadside station characteristic of Antonine organisation, and provided quarters for patrols, signallers or convoy guards. Excavation confirmed that the fort was of the early Antonine period, but the evidence indicated only a single and brief phase of occupation.

The fort is unusual in having an outer parallel enclosure, and in having no man-made defences on

**Raeburnfoot
Roman Fort:
aerial view** (Right)

the steeply scarped western edge. It was once believed that this outer circuit was the original work and that its western defences had been lost to river erosion. However, this natural scarp remains probably much as it was in Roman times, and the two enclosures appear to have been contemporary, the outer one, which yielded no evidence of buildings, possibly having been an annexe.

The site was chosen primarily to suit the inner enclosure. It has a rampart and twin ditches (except on the west), and the interior, which covers an area of about 0.6 ha, contained at least nine wooden buildings, mostly identifiable as barrack blocks. Two of the central group may have had a different, possibly administrative purpose, hence the classification as a small fort rather than a large fortlet; a fortlet is usually made up exclusively of barrack accommodation.

51 Durisdeer, Kirk Burn, Roman Fortlet

1st century AD.

NS 902048. Reached by track from the N end of Durisdeer village (see no. 62), a round trip of more than 3 km on foot.

This fortlet, the best-preserved specimen of its class in the region, stands on a steep-sided ridge guarding the pass through which the Roman road climbs out of Nithsdale. It consists of a single massive rampart, 9 m thick, and an outer ditch, partly rock-cut, and counterscarp bank, all enclosing a rounded oblong area measuring 31.5 m by 18 m. The entrance is at the north-eastern end, and 7.3 m in front of it on the levelled platform is a protective ditch or traverse at least 11 m long. Vestiges of timber structures, probably barrack blocks, have been found inside.

The road, with which this fortlet was associated, may have been in operation in the Flavian era

(AD 85-c 105), but the fortlet itself is one of a number established during the Antonine period after AD 142. Military stations were placed about 16 km apart, much closer together than in the 1st-century occupation, and fortlets such as this housed detachments from the main forts as a means of local control.

52 Burnswark Hill, Fort and Roman Camps

6th century BC-?2nd century AD.

NY 1878, 1879. A minor road runs N to the hill from the B 725 E of Ecclefechan; there is a junction of tracks in the forest plantation at about 213 m OD, and the South Camp lies above the E track on the edge of the plantation.

This great solid table of a hill, visible throughout lower Annandale, is the setting for the most extensive fortification of any kind in the region. Surrounding its twin summits are the ramparts of a native hillfort, covering an area of 7 ha and large enough to have been a major tribal centre. On its northern and southern flanks, carefully planted with an air of calculated menace, are two Roman camps; the larger, southern, camp has three salient artillery platforms, known locally as the 'Three Brethren', thrust purposefully up the hill towards the gateways of the hillfort a mere 120-135 m away. Here the modern visitor can absorb the atmosphere of what looks like an ancient siegework, measure the likely range of the artillery, and gain further insight into that most awesome of war-machines, the Roman military mind.

However, there is no known historical context for such a siege, and these remains probably reflect, not a close encounter between Roman and native, but practice camps for the Roman army in training. Recent excavations have shown that the hillfort defences were not upstanding when lead sling-bolts and stone ballistae balls were being hurled at them; the inference is that Roman troops were using a disused native fort for target practice, leaving the last practice rounds of re-usable ammunition on the hillside for archaeologists to gather up. However, it is not unknown, even within recent times, for such a stage-set for field exercises to grow out of at least one phase of genuine military activity.

Roman Fortlet,
Durisdeer:
aerial view (Left)

**Burnswark Hill:
aerial view**

The main rampart of the hillfort, double on the south east, single on the north, survives in discontinuous stretches of low earthen mounds and terraces. Excavation showed that it dated from around 600 BC, and had a fighting platform set on a double row of timber uprights protected by a stone-built outer face. The three known gateways are in the south-eastern flank. Excavation just above the eastern gate on the edge of the forestry plantation revealed part of the trench of a palisade line which antedates the hillfort. One part of the interior revealed a succession of four timber-built round houses, and hints of native occupation in the late 1st-2nd centuries AD. Other houses are indicated by hilltop hollows and scoops, and it has been estimated that the habitable areas could have contained at least 150 houses at any one time. The earliest identifiable use of the hilltop is marked by a bronze-age cairn and cist burial situated near the centre of the plateau and towards the north-eastern flank. Late use is testified by an artillery redoubt at the south-western end; it probably dates from the mid 17th century and was re-used as a mapping survey station in 1847.

For Roman work, the North Camp is comparatively irregular. It is of linear form, measuring about 305 m in overall length and still preserving much of its rampart and ditch. An outward turn of the rampart protects the gate nearest to the hillfort. The South Camp is a large oblong enclosure some 4.5 ha in area, and its rampart and ditch achieve a substantial overall breadth of 17.7 m on the uphill side. All entrances have been protected by outer mounds of stone-pitched construction, the larger 'Three Brethren' also serving as platforms for ballistae or spring-guns. Embraced within the north-east corner of the camp's defences is a fortlet which can probably be ascribed to the Antonine period about AD 140. Excavations have not provided a date for the practice camps themselves, although the most obvious source of personnel was Birrens (no. 48) which remained in commission as a garrison-post until the AD 180s.

There is no convincing proof of a continuous defensive line around the lower slopes of the hill. The earthwork enclosures east and south west of

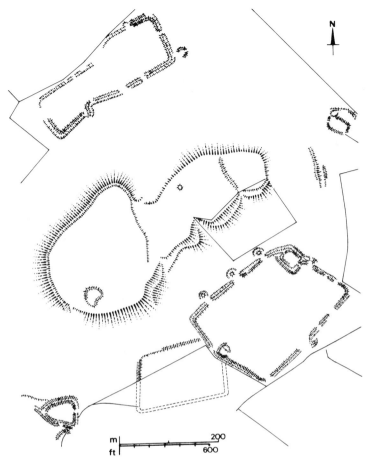

Burnswark Hill: plan

the hill are almost certainly native iron-age settlements, having no apparent defensive or offensive association with the hillfort itself.

53 Ardwell Point, 'Doon Castle', Broch

?1st century AD.

NX 067446. On the A 715 just S of Sandhead, take minor road SW for High Ardwell; access by foot on track from farm at NX 075450, a distance of about 1 km.

A low rocky promontory on the south side of Ardwell Point is host to the best-preserved of the small handful of brochs in western Galloway. The coastal setting is in keeping with such structures, but it is a long way from the main centres of broch-building in northern and north-western Scotland. However, like the outliers in the central Lowlands,

this group does not necessarily reflect a process of migration and colonisation by broch-using peoples; they are more likely to represent the employment by local chieftains, perhaps fearful of Roman military strength, of a class of itinerant broch-engineers.

Compared to some of the mighty drystone towers in the north, the best of the Galloway brochs is a much-reduced specimen, but the essential outlines of its circular design and structural features are clear enough. The interior measures 9 m in diameter with walls 4.6 m in maximum thickness and 1.8 m in greatest height; below this level the entire course of the inner wall-face is still visible. It has been built of large squarish blocks, and at least two cells have been set within the thickness of the wall. There are entrances to seaward and to landward, where the site has been further defended by a transverse wall and a natural gully which is spanned by a stone-faced causeway.

54 'Castle Haven', Dun

1st century BC and medieval.

NX 593482. At Borgue, on the B 727 SE of Gatehouse of Fleet, take minor road W to Corseyard; a footpath skirts the edges of the fields between the road and the shore.

This extraordinary structure, which stands on the rocky foreshore at Kirkandrews, is as much a monument to the energetic enthusiasm of early 20th-century antiquarians as to the needs and aspirations of an iron-age chieftain. It is Galloway's only known example of a galleried dun, a type of fortified homestead common in Argyll and the Western Isles. Castle Haven differs from its cousins of the western seaboard in a number of ways, and first impressions suggest that the height and condition of its drystone walls are one of its distinguishing features. However, its remarkable condition is the result of clearance and restoration work carried out in 1905 by its owner, the laird of Knockbrex, partly with the aim of 'rendering it less liable to be trampled and destroyed than if left in the state in which it was ...'. Before 1905 none of the walls was more than 1.2 m in height, and the west wall, which runs along the rocky edge of Castle Haven Bay, was merely foundations.

Unlike the Argyll duns, this does not preserve evidence of an intra-mural stair; the upper levels were reached by stile-like stone slabs projecting from inner wall faces. The roughly concentric outer enclosure, some 7.3 m in average width, is also an unusual and possibly later feature; it has entrances in the north-eastern and south-eastern sectors, the former corresponding with the main entrances to the inner court.

Although dramatically altering the height of the fortification, the restoration faithfully followed its outline. Backing against the straightish west wall the dun is D-shaped on plan, 18.3 m by 10.7 m in maximum dimensions, with its main entrance in the north-eastern sector; a stepped gateway in the south wall gave access to a boat-landing on the shore below. Within the thickness of the walls there are three narrow galleries of different lengths, which are linked to the interior by no less than six doorways.

The artefacts found in the excavations included bronze spiral finger-rings and a bead of blue glass paste, reflecting sophisticated iron-age origins, whilst pieces of mail and a late type of bronze penannular brooch indicated medieval occupation. There are traditions of an association with the Balliols, and it is possible that in the 14th century the site served as a refuge for Edward Balliol, the last member of the main branch of that family.

55 Rispain Camp

1st century BC and later.

NX 429399. Beyond the end of a farm track off the A 746 1 km SW of Whithorn; cars parked at farm.

Historic Scotland.

This rectangular earthwork on the slope of Camp Hill, north-west of Rispain Farm, is an object-lesson in the perils of archaeological field survey and excavation. Long believed to have been of Roman origin, it was excavated in 1901 but yielded no evidence of date or character. It was later re-classified as a possible medieval moated site, although its size, situation, and deep V-shaped ditch were acknowledged to be untypical. With the assistance of radiocarbon dating techniques, excavations in 1978-81 were able to establish that it was neither Roman nor medieval, but a defended native homestead dating to around 60 BC.

The most impressive visible feature is the surrounding ditch, originally 5.8 m in depth, whose upcast has provided material for earthen banks on each side. Infilled in the south-eastern quarter, the ditch runs almost straight along each side, and a solid bridge of uncut ground, 6.1 m wide, forms the entrance in the north-eastern side. Excavation located a square-cut pit, possibly a water-cistern, in the east corner of the ditch; other ditches and drains around the south and west sides probably related more to field drainage than defence.

Superficially featureless except for traces of a low perimeter bank, the interior covers an area of about 0.35 ha. At the entrance the recent excavations revealed possible evidence for a framed timber gateway, and traces of a metalled road led into the enclosure. An area on the north-western side, roughly one-eighth of the whole, contained at least one circular house, 13.5 m in diameter, and probably originally of post, plank, and ring beam construction. The most noteworthy artefact for dating purposes was an enamelled bronze plate forming part of a bracelet ascribable to the late 1st or 2nd century AD.

56* Castle O'er, Fort

1st millennium BC and later.

NY 241928. From Eskdalemuir on the B 709, take minor road S on W side of the White Esk to Castle O'er farmstead; in forestry plantation 0.7 km NW of farmstead, access restricted.

Forestry Commission.

Keeping at bay a besieging force comprising massed ranks of conifers, the most remarkable of the iron-age hillforts in Eskdale still displays an impressive show of strength. It also continues to pose problems of interpretation as to the nature and sequence of its defences, the numerous linear earthworks in its vicinity, and of the domestic settlement contained within its ramparts.

The earliest phase is probably represented by a half-oval summit area which was defended by a pair of ramparts and intermediate ditch. This enclosure measures 120 m by 60 m, and has always been entered from the east and from the south-west. It was later reduced to corresponding dimensions of 95 m and 35 m upon the construction of a drystone wall in place of the inner rampart; the nine circular house stances visible in the interior are probably contemporary with this phase. Two outer annexes to the south of the fort are enclosed by a system of banks and medial ditches, the outer banks being more pronounced. No credence is now given to the belief that this outer perimeter may have been a Roman siegework.

Hollow-ways run south and east from these outworks, and part of a third linear earthwork survives just to the west of the fort. These form part of an extensive system of 'trenches' recorded in 1896; many appear to have been old tracks and are now absorbed within forestry plantation.

'Kemp's Walk'
Fort: aerial view

57 Kemp's Walk', Fort

Late 1st millennium BC.

NW 975598. W of Stranraer, tracks from the B 738 through Little Larbrax and Meikle Larbrax converge on Larbrax Glen whence there is a climb to the promontory ridge.

Overlooking the sandy expanse of Broadsea Bay at Larbrax, 'Kemp's Walk' is the largest and best-preserved of the promontory forts of western Galloway. On the west side of the northern and only feasible landward approach to the promontory, the defences consist of triple ramparts of soil and gravel with intermediate ditches; on the east side they are reduced to twin ramparts with a medial ditch. There may at one time have been a rampart and outwork around the perimeter of the promontory, except on the west, but there are now no visible traces. In any case, the encircling steep slopes would have afforded considerable natural protection. The interior of the fort measures 83 m by 44.5 m, and extends westwards to a spur crowned by the remains of a circular hut.

58 Barsalloch Point, Fort

Late 1st millennium BC.

NX 347412. Steep ascent by footpath from A 747, S of Port William; signposted.

Historic Scotland.

This promontory fort is situated on the edge of an old sea-cliff in an area which has produced evidence of human encampments early in the 5th millennium BC. At that remote period post-glacial seas washed the base of the cliff, covering the extensive area of raised beach where the modern road runs.

A stiff climb up the steeply sloping heugh is rewarded with the sight of an iron-age fortification whose landward defences consist of a low mounded rampart on each side of an impressive ditch, about 10 m wide overall and 3.5 m in depth. The ditch and ramparts are curved on plan; they back on to the straight side of the cliff and thus form a D-shaped enclosure about 0.1 ha in area. The entrance has been in the north-eastern sector but its position has been partly obscured by a later turf dyke.

59 Mull of Galloway, Earthworks

1st millennium BC.

NX 1430, 1431. The road to the Mull lighthouse crosses both lines of earthworks.

Linear earthworks traverse the Mull of Galloway peninsula on either side of the narrow and low isthmus between East and West Tarbet. The southern line is the longer and bigger of the two, extending over a distance of 400 m from NX 145308 to 141306. For the most part it consists of three ditches with two intermediate banks, the inner and more substantial of the two banks being up to 4 m broad and 2.2 m high. Part of the bank is surmounted by a later turf dyke which blocks four original entrances and makes a right-angled return on top of the western cliffs.

On the opposite side of the isthmus, 330 m north of its partner and immediately south of the enclosed fields, there are traces of a second earthwork reduced to a height of only 0.5 m. It runs from NX 141310 to 142310 along the crest of a natural ridge and partly beneath a modern dyke; at one point there are traces of a stone revetment.

Interpretation of the purpose of these remains gives scope for endless speculation. The isthmus provided boat-sheltering facilities, and a portage for those who wished to avoid the strong tidal races around the point. The Mull itself is a natural citadel, but surviving evidence of man-made activities is confined to a cairn beneath the flagstaff at NX 156304, a cup-marked rock at NX 154304, and the lighthouse (AD 1830), none of which can be equated with these defences.

Mull of Galloway lighthouse and earthworks: aerial view

CHURCHES AND CHRISTIAN MONUMENTS

**Dundrennan Abbey
by Reverend
AB Hutchison,
c1857**

As elsewhere in western Christendom, the seeds of Christianity required a fertile soil in which to germinate, grow, and flourish. The greatest primary aid to that growth and life has always come from lay society which has looked to the Church, in its many different forms, for the fulfilment of its spiritual needs. The nature and direction of its patronage has changed, often dramatically, according to contemporary spiritual values, material wealth, and the Church's own requirements. But, whether erected in times of plenty, or neglected in times of hardship and uncertainty, buildings and commemorative monuments are a telling manifestation of lay support and investment in the affairs of organised religion, and of the Church's view of its many-sided role.

The origins of Christianity in Scotland lie in Galloway. They even antedate the arrival and work, probably in the first half of the 5th century, of Bishop Nynia, a Rome-trained Briton usually better known as St Ninian. The initiative for his appointment almost certainly came from a Christian community requiring the services of a bishop, and his building of a distinctive white church of stone, *Ad Candida Casa*, probably at Whithorn (no. 79), may represent confidence in a settled state of affairs. According to Bede (writing three centuries later), Ninian dedicated his church to St Martin of Tours, and by the 8th century it was believed that, following the pattern established by his alleged mentor, Ninian used a cave (no. 77) as a devotional retreat. Martin's influence and the monastic character of the Ninianic church are matters of scholarly dispute; what is indisputable is the 5th-century date of two inscribed stones at Kirkmadrine (no. 78) and one at Whithorn, the earliest known Christian memorials in Scotland.

Monasticism of the Celtic pattern is thought to have been later established at Whithorn, but its character has eluded archaeological definition. Surprisingly few sites are known to have had enclosed cemeteries and chapels of the type found in Ireland and western mainland Britain; only on Ardwall Isle (NX 573495) has excavation yielded indications of Irish-style shrines and timber chapels of probable late 6th- and 7th-century date.

Kirkmaiden Chapel and churchyard, Monreith

The period of Anglian domination, probably from the early 8th to the early 10th centuries, was marked by a more fruitful source of inspiration from the south and the east. Its outstanding symbol is the Ruthwell Cross (no. 76), which is without equal in Scotland. Ruthwell has no known status as an ecclesiastical centre, but there is evidence of an Anglian monastery or minster at nearby Hoddom (NY 166726), a site closely associated with St Kentigern (d. 612). Hoddom churchyard has been a rich source of Anglian and later sculpture, including portions of two high crosses, now unfortunately lost. Some surviving fragments are in NMS and in Dumfries Museum, which houses Anglian carved pieces from Nithsdale itself (see also no. 75). Northumbrian fashions are also detectable among the crosses at Whithorn, Kirkmadrine and St Ninian's Cave. Whithorn became the centre of an Anglian bishopric in the second quarter of the 8th century, and it is reasonable to suppose that the religious community of scholars known in Kirkcudbright in 1164 had first been established in Anglian times.

The Vikings and the *Gall-Ghaidhils*, forces reckoned to be inimical to the Church, appear to have become receptive to Christian customs, especially in the matter of burial, by the time they settled in Galloway from the 10th century onwards. Scandinavian taste in ornament is evident in some of the late Anglian monuments of the Nithsdale area, and especially in those of the Machars. Their survival in such numbers in this district betokens an era of Christian peace and prosperity in which a luxury trade in funerary monuments could flourish, not only in Whithorn itself, but in outlying centres such as Kirkmaiden (NX 365399), possibly the very first home of the Monreith Cross (now in Whithorn Museum). Two Whithorn crosses bear runic inscriptions, one capable of translation, but otherwise we do not know the identities of the noble patrons who commissioned the crosses and whose graves and cemeteries they marked. Stylistically, Whithorn developed its own school of monumental masonry, characterised by the disc-faced cross. Some stones, most notably the swastika-bearing specimen from Craignarget (now in NMS), betray Cumbrian influence, whilst others are closer to Celtic (eg no. 80) and 'Scottish' traditions (eg the cross-slab from Kilmorie, now at NX 032690).

The bishopric of Whithorn was revived in 1128, and from about 1177 the cathedral was served by a convent of white or Premonstratensian canons, so called because Prémontré, near Laon, in northern France was the head house of the order. Whithorn was one of only two monastic cathedrals in medieval Scotland, the other, St Andrews, having a community of regular clergy of the Augustinian order. At Whithorn the prior and convent shared with the secular clergy of the diocese, not always harmoniously, the privileged duty of electing bishops. And until 1355, long after the independence of the Scottish church had been recognised in 1192, the bishops of Whithorn professed obedience to the metropolitan jurisdiction of the archbishop of York, a fact which increasingly set Whithorn apart from other Scottish dioceses.

Containing 45 parishes at the Reformation in 1560, the medieval diocese covered roughly the area of modern Galloway, except that, from the late 1180s, its eastern boundary was the Urr Water. The bishops of Glasgow had successfully claimed the land between the Urr and the Nith, an area which corresponded with the secular authority of the early sheriffdom of Dumfries. All the parishes east of the Urr (67 by the early 14th century) thus lay in the diocese of Glasgow. From well over 100 medieval parishes, however, only a small proportion has bequeathed remains of parish churches or chapels. An even smaller number, reduced mainly to foundations or fragmentary ruins, can be ascribed to the main period of parish formation in the 12th and 13th centuries. The most complete are the restored Romanesque church at Cruggleton (no. 70) and the Early Gothic structure at Buittle (no. 68). Given the proprietorial nature of early church building, it is no coincidence that these two correspond with principal centres of Galloway lordship.

The main church of the Galloway diocese (no. 79) is itself a somewhat disjointed and enigmatic ruin compared to other Scottish cathedrals of less wealthy sees. Even when complete, Whithorn was almost alone among major Scottish cathedrals in possessing a narrow unaisled nave, although the large and elaborate aisled choir was more appropriate to its status. Soulseat Abbey, from which Whithorn was colonised, was evidently in a ruinous condition by 1386, and has virtually disappeared (NX 100587). Of the other four houses of canons (including two Augustinian), only Tongland (NX 698539) preserves above-ground fragments. Three urban friaries have gone without trace, and two nunneries did not survive the Middle Ages (see no. 66).

More successful, and representative of one of the most successful international business corporations of the Middle Ages, were the three religious houses of the Cistercian order, Dundrennan (no. 73), Glenluce (no. 72), and Sweetheart (no. 71) Abbeys. Their size and sophistication contrast with the poverty of parish church architecture, reflecting an imbalance in patronage and in a financial system based on appropriated parish revenues. Although among the least wealthy of the twelve Scottish houses of this order, and lacking the bulk of their historical records, each of these monasteries has a special claim on visitors' attention. They also deserve more field studies to compensate for the lack of documentation concerning their social and economic background. Cistercian monks were well organised in farming practices, and renowned especially for sheep farming and wool production. Dundrennan is known to have had interests in Balmaclellan in the Glenkens, Galloway's major sheep-run. The moated and settlement sites closer to this abbey (at eg NX 699459, 707501, 717519 and 783572) are unlikely to have been dependent granges, but probably owed much of their social and economic vitality to the Cistercians.

A change in the expression of lay patronage is marked by the Douglas's establishment of Lincluden Collegiate Church (no. 66) in 1389. This was a college of secular priests endowed to celebrate masses for the souls of the founder and his family, a fashion then in vogue among the nobility of western Europe. Such churches, which were in effect private family affairs, fulfilled spiritual needs on a more personal and intimate basis than the increasingly sclerotic monasteries. In an age of conspicuous consumption they also provided an opportunity for a show of secular wealth and status. The eastern limb of the church is of an outstanding richness and quality, and, together with the collegiate church at Bothwell and the failed college at Douglas, gives an indication of the ecclesiastical patronage of the powerful Douglas family. Lincluden also retains the most complete group of associated domestic buildings of any collegiate church in the country, partly an inheritance from its predecessor on the site.

Gordon Monument in Anwoth Church

MacLellan Monument, Greyfriars Church, Kirkcudbright
(Right)

As shown by the principal tomb at Lincluden, elaborate memorials to the dead were sculpted to suit those who could afford to commission them. Outside the major religious houses, however, the region cannot claim a particularly strong tradition in late medieval monumental sculpture. The true heirs to this cult of secular pride are the more fantastic of the post- Reformation effigial tombs such as that which commemorates Sir Thomas MacLellan of Bombie and his wife (1597; see no. 13) in the former church of the Greyfriars in Kirkcudbright. The monument to the 2nd Duke of Queensberry in Durisdeer Church (no. 62) conveys

Kells Churchyard: headstone commemorating John Murray gamekeeper (d. 1777)

a similar impression, and so does the enormous early 17th-century stone sarcophagus of the Gordon family which dominates the interior of Anwoth Old Church (1626; NX 583562). Imagination and skill characterise some of the lesser funerary monuments of the post-Reformation period, and noteworthy groups of table-tombs and headstones can be seen in Dumfries (no. 61), Kirkcudbright (NX 690512), and country churchyards such as Kells (NX 632784).

St Cuthbert's churchyard, Kirkcudbright, table-tomb

However, it is not the quality of stone carving, but the plain and wordy tombstones of the Covenanting era, which give many of the graveyards a special atmosphere. Few of these monuments, or related hilltop memorials, were left untouched by the hand of the itinerant mason-engraver, Robert Paterson (1712-1800), the original of Sir Walter Scott's 'Old Mortality'. He dedicated his working life to the maintenance, re-inscription, and erection of memorials to the victims of the `Killing Times'. He died at Caerlaverock, and there are statues of him and his pony at Dumfries Museum and near the farm at The Holme (NX 646793; formerly in Balmaclellan village).

Statue of Robert Paterson ('Old Mortality') and his pony, Dumfries Museum

The Covenanters, so called because of their subscription to the National Covenant of 1638, were strongest and most extreme in Ayrshire and the South West. It was here that pro-presbyterian, anti-episcopal sentiment showed itself most openly among dissident ministers and their communities following the re-introduction of bishops in 1662. Their resistance took the form of open rebellion, guerilla activities, and attendance at open-air gatherings or conventicles. In an atmosphere loaded with sectarian hatred and suspicions of treason, the government carried out heavy-handed military and judicial reprisals, particularly after 1681, and mainly through Graham of Claverhouse operating from Stranraer Castle (no. 15) and Sir Robert Grierson of Lag, owner of Rockhall (no. 27). The 80 summary executions that were witnessed in 1684-5 were probably only a proportion of the whole, but of all these the martyrdom of young Margaret Wilson at Wigtown (no. 63) was undoubtedly the most notorious. The last of the martyrs was James Renwick, executed in February 1688, and his monument stands just west of Moniaive, a centre for hill-country conventicles.

On Skeoch Hill at NX 859791 a memorial and four parallel rows of stones, the 'Communion Stones', mark the setting of a 3,000-strong gathering in 1679. Even more remote is a 1681 conventicle site at Blackgannoch

(NS 754174) among the hills to the north of Sanquhar, an area where a remnant of the Covenanters (known as Cameronians) remained faithful to 'true' presbyterianism after the establishment of the Presbyterian Church of Scotland in 1690. It was in Nithsdale that Daniel Defoe was witness to an old Cameronian preaching 'to an auditory of near 7,000 people, all sitting in rows on the steep side of a green hill, and the preacher in a little pulpit made under a tent at the foot of the hill; he held his auditory, with not above an intermission of half an hour, almost seven hours and many of the poor people had come fifteen or sixteen miles to hear him, and had all the way to go home again on foot'.

Religious and political circumstances, clearly, were not propitious for much church building until after 1690 (see eg nos 61, 62), and in the Border areas physical damage from warfare had to be made good. The most ambitious of the few early 17th-century church-building schemes was that funded by Viscount Montgomery at Portpatrick (no. 64). In the meantime, as the Protestant Reformation ran its rough and often bitter course between 1560 and 1690, old beliefs and practices lingered on. Remarkable for the fact that it was built by a Roman Catholic family within a generation of the Reformation is the choir of Terregles Parish Church (no. 65; see also no. 71). Despite the fact that freedom of worship was not permitted until after 1779 and the ban on civil liberties not removed until 1829, adherence to the old faith persisted covertly, usually under the protective aegis of leading Catholic families such as the Maxwells (no. 60). The force of their traditions, religious convictions, and community spirit was no doubt just as great as those which conditioned diehard Covenanters. In the history of religious beliefs, Dumfries and Galloway has a remarkably ancient, proud, and staunch record.

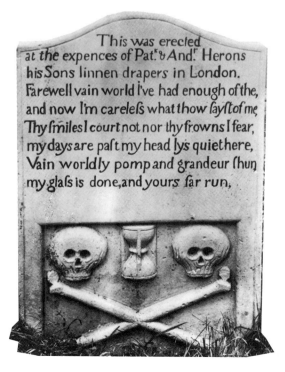

This was erected at the expences of Pat.ʳ ᵇ And.ʳ Herons his Sons linnen drapers in London.
Farewell vain world I've had enough of the, and now I'm careleſs what thow ſayſt of me, Thy ſmiles I court not nor thy frowns I fear, my days are paſt my head lys quiet here, Vain worldly pomp and grandeur ſhun my glaſs is done, and yours far run,

Headstone,
Wigtown
churchyard

60 St Peter's RC Church, Dalbeattie

AD 1814.

NX 831613. To the NW of the A 711, W of the town centre.

Attention is drawn to this little granite church, not because of any outstanding architectural merit, but because, alongside St Andrew's, Dumfries, it marks the physical re-emergence of native Catholicism in areas where adherence to the old faith had persisted since the Reformation. In this case, successive domestic chaplains of the Maxwells of nearby Munches (NX 830589) had served the needs of a satellite community, and after the death in 1809 of Agnes, the last Catholic member of the family, the incumbent, Father Andrew Carruthers, a native of New Abbey, used a portion of her bequest to establish a church and priest's house in the rising village of Dalbeattie. The oldest church in Dalbeattie, it was built in 1814 to seat 252 persons, extensive alterations and repairs having been undertaken in 1935 and in more recent times.

Durisdeer Church: monument to the 2nd Duke of Queensberry, and columns of baldacchino in foreground

61 St Michael's Church and Churchyard, Dumfries

AD 1745; monuments 17th century and later.

NX 975757. On the S side of the A 75 by-pass at the intersection with the B 725 (St Michael's Street).

Large and dominant, this Georgian hall church with its Gothic-like spire occupies the site of a medieval burgh church, whose dedication (to St Michael) it inherits. The gatepiers at the entrance to the churchyard are hollow, equipped with halved doors, and served as elders' sentry-boxes. The churchyard itself is well stocked with a variety of funerary monuments, many demonstrating the versatile and tractable qualities of the local red sandstone. Towards the eastern end there is the mausoleum in the form of a rotunda beneath which the remains of Robert Burns were re-interred in 1815. Nearby, a tall granite obelisk of 1834 marks an area of Covenanters' tombstones, restored in 1873, whose lengthy inscriptions convey the bitter sectarian spirit of the 'Killing Times' in the 17th century.

62 Durisdeer Church

c AD 1699.

NS 893037. At centre of village which is clearly signposted from the A 702.

Somewhat unexpected in its moorland village setting, this building is of a size and quality above that of the average Scottish rural parish kirk. It owes this superiority to the patronage of the Queensberry family of Drumlanrig (no. 25), and its most distinguished feature is the family's burial-aisle on the north side of the church. Ashlar-built and ogival-roofed, this Baroque creation is marble-floored inside and contains a white marble baldacchino (canopy) placed over the entrance to the burial-vault of the 1st Duke of Queensberry, builder of Drumlanrig. This was designed by James Smith, architect, whilst the mural monument in the north wall to the 2nd 'Union' Duke and his wife was carved in 1713 by the Anglo-Dutch sculptor, John van Nost. The church itself, dated 1699 on a sundial above the south door, is of a cruciform plan with a former school building at the west end. The tall timber spire of its central tower was removed in the 19th century.

The churchyard monuments include a table-tomb to Daniel McMichael, a Covenanter killed in 1685, and a headstone, also of 1685, which commemorates four children of William Lukup, Master of Works at Drumlanrig. The stone bears the relief-carved effigy of a mason holding a mell and a chisel.

63 Martyrs' Tomb, Wigtown

AD 1685.

NX 435555. The churchyard is on the E side of the town below the main central square.

One of the most infamous groups of Covenanting tombstones, all dating from 1685 and bearing later inscriptions, is contained within a railed enclosure in the northern half of the burial-ground at Wigtown. The lengthy text of the single table-tomb commemorates the sad fate of the 18-year old Margaret Wilson, who was martyred by drowning 'within the sea tied to a stake'. A headstone records that Margaret Lachlan, aged 63, suffered likewise, and a second headstone refers to the hanging 'without sentence of law' of William Johnston, John Milroy, and George Walker 'for their adherence to Scotland's Reformation Covenant's National and Solemn League'. In 1858 a martyrs' monument in the form of an obelisk was erected on Windyhill (430554), and a stone post at NX 437556 marks the approximate site of the drowning, now dry land.

64 Old Parish Church, Portpatrick

c AD 1629.

NW 999542. Churchyard entered from Saint Patrick Street, a W loop of Main Street

The four-stage circular tower of this ruinous church is conspicuous in the centre of Portpatrick, and was probably designed to serve both as a belfry and navigational beacon for the early harbour (no. 1). The shell of the church to which it is attached is of an equal-armed cruciform plan, and is dated on the gable skewput (the lowest stone), 1629; a screen-wall was subsequently built across the western aisle to form a T-plan interior. The church was lit by lintelled and mullioned windows in each of the

Portpatrick Old Parish Church: inner face of tower

three gables, and above them on the outer walls are spaces for carved panels. Moulded fragments, possibly from a medieval chapel on this site, have been reused in the building fabric. Prior to the current scheme of restoration and consolidation, the tower was repaired in about 1880, and the church last used for worship in 1842 when the present parish church was built.

Some of the tombstones in the burial-ground commemorate the maritime tragedies which have beset Portpatrick, the most poignant perhaps being that to the fifty victims of the wrecked steamship, Orion, in 1850.

65 Terregles Church and 'Queir'

AD 1583.

NX 930770. Churchyard reached from lane at Kirkland, the S portion of Terregles village.

At the eastern end of this small parish church is the 'queir' (choir), built as a mortuary chapel by the 4th Lord Herries in 1583. Its special significance lies in the fact that it was erected in the immediate post-Reformation era by a Roman Catholic family, and that, with its mixture of pointed and round-headed openings and three-sided apse, it perpetuates some of the traditional Gothic forms of the later Middle Ages. The existing church was built in 1799 on the site of an earlier nave. The buttresses, window tracery and much of the interior of the choir date from a restoration carried out by Captain Maxwell of Terregles in 1875. Inside, at the foot of the staircase leading to the burial-vault, there is a large slab monument of 1568 bearing a male effigy in contemporary costume.

Terregles 'Queir'

Lincluden Collegiate Church

66* Lincluden Collegiate Church

Early 15th century AD.

NX 966779. Signposted from A 76 through housing estate on N outskirts of Dumfries.

Historic Scotland.

This precious gem of medieval architectural and social history stands close to the confluence of the Cluden Water and the River Nith. There are two distinct elements: the choir, south transept and fragment of the nave of an elegant collegiate church, and, extending northwards from the church sacristy, a rubble-built domestic and service range. On the east, the layout includes a restored formal knot garden and, immediately to the south, a tree-shrouded and terraced motte, which has obviously been part of the horticultural scheme.

How long the early castle mound remained in use for serious defensive purposes is not known, for a Benedectine nunnery was founded here, evidently by Uchtred (d. 1174), son of Fergus, Lord of Galloway. The nunnery was said to have been endowed to support up to ten nuns, but at the date of its suppression in 1389 it housed only four. In his papal petition to abolish the nunnery and erect in its place a collegiate church, Archibald, 3rd Earl of Douglas, claimed that the nuns lived 'disgracefully'; they 'do not trouble to repair the beautiful buildings, ... which are disfigured and ruinous through their sloth and neglect, but deck with fine clothing and ornaments their daughters born of their immoralities whom they rear in common with them in the same monastery'.

His allegations were seemingly sustained, and authority was granted for the establishment of a college of secular priests whose main job would be to celebrate masses for the souls of the founder and his family. The staff of the college comprised a provost and eight prebendaries (priests), later increased to twelve, together with 24 bedesmen to serve the annexed poors' hospital at Holywood.

It is Douglas wealth which is now so sumptuously displayed in the surviving architecture and sculpture, but the claustral layout of the nunnery guided the planning of the collegiate establishment. Authorship of the architecture may be attributed to John Morow, a Parisian-born master-mason whose work at Melrose Abbey was accompanied by an inscribed panel listing other Scottish commissions, including work in 'Nyddysdayl' (Nithsdale). The forms of the stone mouldings and window tracery show close affinities with Melrose, and would have coincided with the acquisition of French tastes and interests by the founder's son, Archibald, 4th Earl of Douglas and Duke of Touraine, who was killed at Verneuil in 1424. It is the effigy and tomb of his

Merkland Cross

widow, Princess Margaret, eldest daughter of King Robert III, which takes pride of place on the north side of the choir, and her status is denoted by the magnificence of the tomb surround. Similar craftsmanship is also shown in the surround of the adjacent sacristy door, and of the sedilia and piscina in the opposite wall. There is indeed a wealth of testimony to the stone-carver's art: note especially the ubiquitous heraldry, the angel-musicians at the bases of the vaulting-ribs, and the enriched cornice of the stone choir screen, itself a rare survival. A relief-sculptured panel portraying the Apostles was originally set on the parapet or rood loft above this screen and is now preserved in one on the vaults of the domestic range.

The southern half of the domestic block, originally three-storeyed and known as the Provost's Lodging, was probably built in the first half of the 15th century. The projecting stair-tower and the northern half of the range, which included a four-storeyed tower, is believed to have been the work of Provost William Stewart (1529-36). This range continued in use as a residence into the second half of the 17th century.

67 Merkland Cross, Woodhouse

15th century AD.

NY 250721. In a field above a farm road, close to its junction with the A 74, 8 km NW of Gretna Green.

Historic Scotland.

This late medieval wayside cross stands 3 m high, has a floriated head, and is apparently monolithic; the base is modern. What it actually commemorates is not so easily described. There are at least three versions of a tradition in which a military commander is reputed to have been slain here in unusual circumstances, the least implausible of which relates to the death of John, Master of Maxwell, in the running fight with the Duke of Albany's supporters which started in Lochmaben in July 1484. However, there is no evidence that there were any Maxwells present in that battle, and the Master of Maxwell is known to have been slain in a family feud by Murray of Cockpool.

Buittle Churches and Churchyard: aerial view

Buittle Old Parish Church: chancel arch and east windows (Far right)

68 Buittle, Old Parish Church

13th and 14th centuries AD.

NX 807598. Churchyard entered from lane, a short distance S of the A 745, SE of Castle Douglas.

The roofless shell of the most intact medieval parish church in the region stands in the churchyard at Buittle to the south of its 19th-century successor. It consists of a plain unaisled nave to which a wider and more elaborate chancel has been added. The nave possibly belongs to the 13th century, while the belfry and other minor alterations are post-Reformation products. The east wall of the chancel has an array of three single-light windows, beneath which there is a later central doorway. The form of the chancel arch, and the heads of the window embrasures indicate perhaps a late 13th- or early 14th-century date.

This church may date substantially from the era of Balliol lordship of Buittle between 1234 and 1296, but the chancel may belong to the period of Douglas possession after 1325. In 1347 the parish and its church were appropriated by the abbot and convent of Sweetheart Abbey. It remained in use until the present parish church was built in 1819. There is a tradition, first recorded in 1684, that the church of this parish was originally at Kirkennan (NX 8258) where remains of burials, but not buildings, have been found.

69 St Ninian's Chapel, Isle of Whithorn

c AD 1300.

NX 479362. Signposted and car park in village; footpath from S end of village to isthmus of headland.

Historic Scotland.

This neat little building, first restored and partly rebuilt in 1898, stands close to a rocky inlet on the seaward side of the Isle of Whithorn, once a genuine island but now a promontory linked to the mainland by Harbour Row and its associated quay. It is conceivable that it occupies a site associated with St Ninian, but no Early Christian remains have been recorded from the island. Excavations located the foundations of a narrower chancel, probably of 12th-century date, but nothing older. As it stands, the chapel and its enclosure-wall date from about 1300 when it was rebuilt as a single structural chamber with a south doorway, a two-light east window, and smaller windows in the side-walls. Much of the dressed stonework is modern. In 1864 it was reported that 'a certain retired sea-captain ... took out the dressed stones some years

St Ninian's Chapel, Isle of Whithorn

ago to help up his house in the village'. A pre-restoration sketch of 1887 shows that the embrasure of the despoiled east window was of distinctly pointed form.

In the Middle Ages the chapel probably served the resident community at the port of Whithorn, as well as pilgrims arriving by sea from Ireland and Man.

is laid out on a simple two-chambered plan, with nave and narrower chancel.

Which of the 12th century lords of Galloway was responsible for this work is not known, although the strongest claims have been made in favour of Fergus (d. 1161). In 1427 its modest revenues were appropriated by the Bishop of Whithorn, and in the 17th century the small parish was united with that of Sorbie. The apparent physical isolation of the church may be deceptive, although no traces of a village settlement have been found in its vicinity.

70 Cruggleton Church

12th century AD.

NX 477428. E of Whithorn in walled enclosure in cultivated field E of the B 7063. Check at Cruggleton Farm; parking restricted.

Reflecting the patronage of the lords of nearby Cruggleton Castle (NX 484429) and the architectural influence of Whithorn (no. 79), this is the most complete small Romanesque church in the region. In its existing form, however, the building is largely the product of a scheme of restoration carried out in about 1890 on what was then a ruin, a line of tiles marking the base of the rebuilt work. Outside, the character of the original masonry and doorway can best be seen on the north side; of the windows only the small east and west single-light openings are old. Inside, there is an original chancel arch which has been partly reset; it has a pair of shafted orders with cubical and scalloped capitals and Irish-style bulbous bases. The church

Cruggleton Church: chancel arch

Sweetheart Abbey: aerial view

Nave, crossing-tower and east window (Far right)

Effigy of foundress, Dervorguilla de Balliol (Bottom right)

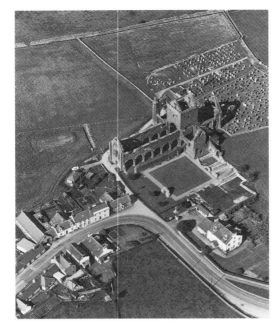

71* Sweetheart Abbey

Late 13th and 14th centuries AD.

NX 965662. Signposted on the A 710 and situated at the E end of New Abbey village.

Historic Scotland.

Of red Nithsdale sandstone and hugely, but fittingly, out of scale with the village, the abbey church of Sweetheart or New Abbey ('new' in relation to the mother-house of Dundrennan) was the last, and is now the most complete, of Galloway's trio of Cistercian monasteries. It is also the most romantic. Its name, 'Dulce Cor' (Sweetheart), reflects the circumstances of its foundation in 1273 by the rich and pious Dervorguilla de Balliol in fond memory of her husband, John (d. 1268). His embalmed heart in a casket was buried with her on her death in 1290. An effigy of the foundress bearing a representation of the heart casket surmount the reassembled fragments of a copy of her tomb in the south transept chapel.

Anglo-Scottish warfare evidently delayed building works in the later 13th and 14th centuries, and caused much damage to the abbey's property. Its buildings were also struck by lightning before 1381, and were alleged in 1397 to have been 'totally burned'. At the Reformation in 1560 it was staffed by an abbot and convent of 15 monks, and, covertly, under Maxwell family protection, Roman rites continued into the early 17th century. The abbey and its estates were formed into a secular lordship in 1624, but successive buildings in and around the cloister continued to serve as the parish church until 1877. Positive affection for the abbey church ensured its survival, for in 1779 it was purchased from the owners and would-be quarriers of the site by a local consortium 'desirous of preserving the remainder of that building as an ornament to that part of the country'; the conventual buildings were practically all removed, however, leaving only the gateway from the outer court into the cloister.

Opinions differ as to the quality of the design and detailing of the church itself; its unquestioned merits are its colour and its completeness. Virtually all load-bearing medieval masonry is still in place except for parts of the transepts and the outer wall of the north nave-aisle. Its layout demonstrates the essential conservatism of Cistercian planning: a cruciform outline consisting of aisled nave, square-ended transepts (with a pair of chapels in each transept) and simple unaisled chancel. The structural nave, in this case two-storeyed and of six bays, contained the liturgical choirs required for lay brothers and monks. The provision of a low belfry-tower over the crossing and the introduction of decorative details, particularly in the traceried windows, represent departures from earlier and stricter Cistercian practice. There are rose windows in the west and south gables, the latter encircling, halo-like, a solid segment of the roof apex of the former east range. The surviving bar tracery involves much use of geometric circles, a style well exemplified in the great east window.

Outside the churchyard, the abbey precincts are enclosed on the north and east sides by a massive granite boulder-built wall up to 3.6 m high and 1.2 m wide, one of the most complete of its kind in the country. The wall originally embraced an area of more than 12 hectares, the site of the western gateway being marked by a roadside pillar in the middle of the modern village. The eastern wall is reduced to footings, and the southern boundary was apparently formed by a water-filled ditch.

 Glenluce Abbey

72* Glenluce Abbey

13th and 15th centuries AD.

NX 185586. Signposted from the A 75 at the curve W of Glenluce village; it lies about 2 km N on the New Luce road.

Historic Scotland and NTS.

Laid out on the river plain of the Water of Luce, the ruins of Glenluce Abbey have the remote setting, the tranquil atmosphere, and plain austerity originally associated with the monastic ideals of Citeaux and its colonies. Glenluce was founded in 1191/2 by Roland, Lord of Galloway, as a daughter-house of Dundrennan, but little is known of its institutional history. In the 16th century its buildings and possessions were prey to the conflicting ambitions of local landed families, most notably the Gordons of Lochinvar and the Earls of Cassillis, through their protégés, the Hays of Park (see no. 29). In 1560 it had a complement of 16 regular monks, including the abbot and prior, but ordinarily the number, excluding lay brothers, may have been closer to 20. The monastery was formally secularised in 1602.

The slight remains of the abbey church, which lies across the northern end of the site, match our scant knowledge of its history. Except for the south transept, it is reduced mainly to wall-footings. The layout is clear enough, however, and conforms to the usual Cistercian model: aisled nave, sizeable transepts, each with a pair of chapels, and a simple unaisled and square-ended presbytery. The surviving piers and bases are reminiscent of the

**Dundrennan
Abbey: aerial view**
(Right)

Effigy of abbot
(Lower right)

link, through Dundrennan, with the building styles of Byland and Roche Abbeys in Yorkshire. The floor was tiled, and there are noteworthy monuments to the Gordons and to the Hays, rivals even in the commemoration of death. From the corner of the south transept the night stair ascended to the monks' dormitory on the upper floor, and a doorway led through to the sacristy. The adjacent inner parlour formed a tile-floored passage from the cloister to the burial-ground on the east.

The southern half of the east range was rebuilt in the latter half of the 15th century, and includes the chapter house, the abbey's main surviving claim to architectural distinction. The capitals of its moulded doorway bear foliaceous, seaweed-like carving. The interior, 7.3 m square, is roofed with a four-compartment ribbed vault springing from a central shafted pier. Part of the original tiled floor still survives, and the stone bench-seat for conventual meetings runs around the wall; the abbot's stall was at the centre of the east wall between a pair of traceried windows.

Beyond the cellars at the end of the east range is the base of the reredorter, or latrines-block, formerly associated with the monks' dormitory on the floor above. The building set at right angles to the south side of the cloister is the original refectory; it was subdivided in the 16th century to form the service basement of a domestic residence with a detached kitchen to the west. The western range of the cloister garth originally provided accommodation for the ancillary staff of lay brothers. The water-supply system is a rare, possibly unique, survival, retaining as it does the jointed earthenware pipes and lidded junction-boxes at the base of the drainage-channels.

73* Dundrennan Abbey

Mid and later 12th century AD.

NX 749475. Below the A 711 in the centre of Dundrennan village; signposted.

Historic Scotland.

Although a mere fragment of its former grandeur, the architecture of Dundrennan Abbey is the most

accomplished piece of medieval workmanship in the province. The first two of its three main building phases are almost a text-book demonstration of the transition from round-arched Romanesque to pointed Early Gothic styles. How building work of this quality was organised and funded in the heart of semi-independent Galloway in the middle and later decades of the 12th century are questions to which we can only dimly perceive the answers. Its foundation in about 1142 as a daughter-house of Rievaulx Abbey in Yorkshire must have been to the mutual political advantage of King David I, Fergus, Lord of Galloway, and the Cistercians themselves.

A letter of 1165 refers to Dundrennan 'as the abbey which the brethren of Rievaulx built', no doubt perpetuating the skills developed in the completion of the church at Rievaulx itself. The later 12th-century work, however, shows closer stylistic affinities with other Yorkshire Cistercian monasteries, and these operations were presumably afforded by the wealth of its own estate. It probably enjoyed a generous landed endowment (including lands in Ireland) from the native lords of Galloway, the last of whom, Alan (d. 1234), was buried here, but our knowledge of the abbey's history is negligible. We can only infer that the creation of two further major dependencies (nos 71, 72) shows that Galloway was to the Cistercians' liking.

The last stages of the monastery's existence are better charted: in 1529 the abbey buildings were reputedly in a state of collapse, and at the Reformation in 1560 the convent comprised at least twelve monks. The ownership of the abbey and its estate was fully secularised in 1606 when it was formed into a lordship for John Murray, later 1st Earl of Annandale.

Like many monastic ruins, Dundrennan demands an effort of imaginative reconstruction. The gateway through which the visitor enters the abbey precincts used to be the central doorway at the west end of an 8-bay aisled nave, now reduced mainly to its foundations. Those portions that survive practically to full height are the north and south transept and adjacent portions of the unaisled chancel. These tell us that the first church was two-storeyed, incorporating a range of clerestorey (upper level) windows. The crossing, the eastern walls of the transepts, and the chapels behind them, were then remodelled in the last quarter of the 12th century. Giant three-bay arcades gave access to the chapels which were redesigned with rib-vaulted ceilings; above the arcades a triforium (middle) stage was introduced, the refined and spacious effect being a step further away from original ascetic ideals. Primary and secondary work alike was wrought in ashlar masonry of local extraction.

Of the claustral buildings only parts of the east and west ranges are now clearly visible. Their chief glory is the late 13th-century arcaded frontage of the chapter house which has a cusped doorway and flanking two-light windows. It possessed a grand aisled and vaulted interior, sub-divided into twelve vaulted compartments. The west range, like that at Glenluce (no. 72) originally provided all the accommodation and services required by the community of lay brothers, but at a late stage was rebuilt to form a series of vaulted cellars. Parts of the cloister arcade are among the architectural fragments housed in the vaults.

Early and mainly abbatial grave-slabs, including those with matrices for brasses, have been set into the renewed floor of the chapter house. Two other monuments found in the chapter house, one an effigy of an abbot and the other (dated 1480) commemorating a cellarer, have been mounted in a recess, formerly a doorway, at the north-west end of the nave. A tomb recess at the north end of the north transept contains a mutilated effigy of a knight, possibly of 13th-century date and said to represent Alan of Galloway.

74 Chapel Finian, Mochrum

10th or 11th century AD.

NX 278489. On side of A 747, NW of Port William, signposted.

Historic Scotland.

The foundations of this small rectangular chapel lie close to the coastal road and the shore on the old raised beach at Corwall Port. Oriented east-west, it has a south doorway and there are three buttresses on each of the side-walls, one in the centre and one against each corner. Excavation revealed evidence of a stone bench, possibly encased in wood, set against the inner eastern face of the south wall. The mortared masonry includes use of large upright stones set on edge to form foundation-courses and door-jambs. The building is tightly enclosed within the footings of a drystone boundary wall, and a stone-lined well lies outside, close to the entrance-gateway in the roadside dyke.

Chapel Finian

Cross-shaft, Nith Bridge

In 1684 this building was described as 'a little ruinous chapel call'd by the country people Chapel Finzian'. It probably takes its name from St Finian of Moville (Co. Down, Ulster), who was educated at Whithorn and died in about 579. The site may mark an episode in the life of the saint, and it may have been a landing-place for Irish pilgrims to St Ninian's shrine.

75 Nith Bridge, Cross-shaft, Thornhill

10th century AD.

NX 868954. In field immediately S of the A 702 and W of the river bridge.

Next to Ruthwell, this is the most complete Anglian sculptured cross in the region. Standing to an overall height of 2.7 m, it remains intact except for the top and side-arms of the cross-head and may occupy its original position. The cross-head had double concave 'arm-pits' with a flat central rosette. The faces are made up of zoomorphic-carved panels, including paired and winged beasts, while the narrow sides bear continuous variegated plait decoration.

76* Ruthwell Cross

Early 8th century AD.

NY 100682. Inside Ruthwell Parish Church, some 9 km W of Annan; key available at the modern house (NY 100681) near the B 724.

Historic Scotland.

This is the most important Anglian cross in Scotland and a monument of international reputation. It stands 5.2 m high at the sunken centre of a semicircular apse specially erected for the purpose in 1887. Between 1823 and 1887 it stood at the gateway to the manse, reassembled from broken pieces which since 1642 had lain first in the clay floor of the church and then in the churchyard. As 'an idolatrous monument' it had been partly defaced, broken, and buried in order to comply with the wishes of a General Assembly in 1640. At that date, and at its first recorded mention in 1600, the cross stood inside the church. The effaced and broken portions, and the modern insertions (including the transom, ie the bar of the cross-head), are clearly visible, but the magnificence of the design and its detailing transcend the damage and the structural surgery.

Its significance, however, goes beyond the quality of the composition and its execution. It has, in the words of Professor Rosemary Cramp, 'the most complete theological programme of any surviving cross', and illustrates more perfectly than any other 'the intellectual background of Northumbrian Christianity'. It does this by coherent schemes of words and pictures: on the broad faces there are panels of carved figures and marginal texts, virtually all in Latin; the narrow sides have vinescrolls inhabited by birds and beasts and runic-inscribed margins. The panels and Latin texts describe and illustrate the divinity and power of Christ; the animated scrolls and the runes are related to the theme of Creation, the text being a precursor of the Anglo-Saxon poem, 'The Dream of the Rood'.

The symbolism of the carvings, suggestions about its missing pieces, the source of the design and its carvers, and its probable date, are subjects which have given rise to enough scholarly literature to paper the walls of the kirk. Suffice to say that current opinion is in favour of an early or mid 8th-century date, its closest but less homogeneous and possibly slightly earlier parallel being Bewcastle Cross in Cumbria. The style and the iconography of the two crosses may have been derived from Eastern Mediterranean models, probably through master carvers trained in one of the great monastic houses of Northumbria, perhaps from the area that is now Yorkshire. The meanings of the carvings and the texts also make clear sense in relation to the liturgical calendar and practices of contemporary Northumbria. The veneration of the Cross was important in the Northumbrian version of Roman liturgy, especially after Pope Sergius's miraculous finding of a relic of the True Cross in 701, an event which may have inspired the erection of the Bewcastle and Ruthwell Crosses.

The north, probably originally the west, face has as its central panel the figure of Christ in Majesty with his feet resting on the heads of a pair of animals. The surrounding text reads: 'Jesus Christ the judge of equity. The animals and the serpents

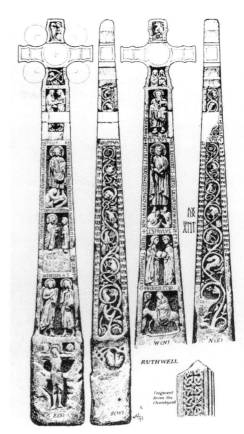

Drawing by WG Collingwood, 1917

Ruthwell Cross in the churchyard prior to 1887
(Above left)

recognised the Saviour of the world in the desert'. The panel immediately above depicts St John the Baptist holding the Lamb, and the associated incomplete text reads 'we worship'. The corresponding panel below shows the two hermit saints, Paul and Anthony, the inscription St Paul and A(nthony) broke bread in the desert', the whole scene being an allusion to the Holy Mass. The lowest visible panel shows the Flight into Egypt with Mary and Child seated on an ass; the remains of the superscription read 'Mary and Jo(seph) ...'. The larger panel at the base, which has been effaced, possibly bore a representation of the Nativity.

On the south face, the central panel shows Mary Magdalene washing the feet of Christ, with an almost complete quotation: 'she brought an alabaster box of ointment; and standing behind (beside) his feet, she began to moisten his feet with tears, and with the hairs of her own head she wiped (them)' (Vulgate Luke 7:37-8). The panel beneath represents the Healing of the Blind Man, and a fragment of the text 'And passing by (He) saw (blind) from birth' (John 9:1). Below is a representation of the Annunciation with a vestige of text from Luke 1:28 'The angel came in ...'. The much-damaged panel at the foot bore a Crucifixion scene. The Visitation is shown towards the upper end of the shaft above the Magdalene relief; it is surrounded by a runic, not Latin, text, part of which can be understood to mean 'Mary, mother of

the Lord'. The panel immediately below the arm contains an archer, and a pair of unidentified figures occupy a corresponding position on the other side.

The head of the cross, apparently replaced the wrong way round, bears on one side an eagle as a symbol of the Ascension, and, on the other, St John the Evangelist and his emblem, also an eagle. The runic texts on the sides have been translated and reconstructed in the following passages: '....God almighty stripped himself when he wanted to ascend the cross, brave before men ...; ... I (bore) the noble King, the Lord of Heaven, I did not dare bow; men mocked us both together; I was smeared with blood ...; ... Christ was on the cross; yet there eager noble men came from afar to him alone; I beheld all that; I was sorely troubled with sorrows ...; ... They laid him wounded with arrows, weary in limb; they stood at the head of his body, they beheld there ...'.

---

77 St Ninian's Cave

8th century AD and later.

NX 422359. Signposted from A 747, S of Whithorn, at Physgill; car park at Kidsdale whence a 1.8 km walk to the cave, the last 400 m being along a stony beach to the west of Physgill Glen.

Historic Scotland.

St Ninian's Cave

A cleft in the headland at the northern end of the Physgill shore is part of a collapsed cave which since 1871 has been the scene of some remarkable archaeological discoveries. By tradition, this south-facing cave was long regarded as a devotional retreat used by St Ninian. The discovery of crosses incised on the face of the living rock, and on loose boulders and slabs confirmed that veneration of the cave goes back at least to the 8th century when Galloway was under Northumbrian influence. Most of these crosses are probably votive, cut by pilgrims to record their visit and their offering made in honour of the saint.

Between points 6 m outside the cave and 3 m from its inner end there are seven small crosses incised on the western rock-face. The forms of the crosses suggest an 8th- or 9th-century date, the outermost one perhaps even earlier. Excavations conducted between 1883 and 1886 brought to light among the debris of the collapsed cave a number of loose stones bearing votive crosses, two pillar stones, and a sculptured Anglian headstone carved with interlace ornament and part of a runic inscription. About eleven stones are ascribable to the 11th century or earlier, and all are now in Whithorn Museum. Among other items recovered from the cave is an inscribed slate dedicated to St Ninian, the lettering having probably been scratched in post-Reformation times.

Stone pavements and fragmentary walls represented relatively modern occupation-levels and were lifted in 1950. The early floor had been destroyed, but from the positions of the rock-incised crosses it evidently stood at much the same level as it does today.

78 Kirkmadrine (Rhins), Early Christian Stones

5th century AD and later.

NX 080483. Follow signposts from A 716 S of Sandhead.

Historic Scotland.

Displayed in a glass-fronted porch of a late 19th-century burial chapel at Kirkmadrine are the oldest Christian monuments in Scotland outside Whithorn. The most informative and oldest of the group, a pillar stone which dates from the 5th century, bears a six-line Latin inscription: 'Here lie the holy and chief priests (ie Bishops), Ides, Viventius and Mavorius', and, at the top, above a circled cross 'A(lpha) and (Omega)'. The incised equal-armed cross has a crooked loop on the upper arm, signifying the sacred *chi-rho* monogram. A similar cross and symbol are formed on a second pillar, presumably of later 5th-century date, which

Kirkmadrine Chapel: 5th century pillar stone (Far right)

Pillar stone of *c* AD 600

is more enigmatically inscribed '(Here lie) ... s and Florentius'. A smaller pillar stone has the Latin inscription, 'The beginning and the end', a variant of the Alpha and Omega symbol as defined in Revelation 21:6. The form of the cross and the style of lettering suggest a date of around AD 600. The other funerary monument on display include five cross-fragments which range in date from the 8th to the 12th centuries.

When first discovered in the 19th century the three oldest pillar stones were serving as gateposts and as a stile-slab in the churchyard wall; the rest were found in the churchyard itself. Collectively, they represent an early Christian cemetery of some importance in this neighbourhood. Unfortunately, nothing is otherwise known about the identity and authority of these bishop-priests; presumably they served Christian communities in this area, perhaps as an offshoot from Whithorn (no. 79). The compound name, Kirkmadrine, implies a dedicatory saint, usually taken to be St Mathurinus, but the name is not recorded before 1500. The medieval parish was known as Toskerton and was united with Stoneykirk in 1618. Lady McTaggart Stewart of Ardwell had the chapel rebuilt in neo-Romanesque style out of the medieval ruins on the site, modelling it on Cruggleton (no. 70).

Whithorn: aerial view

79* Whithorn, Early Christian Monastery, Cathedral-Priory and Stones

5th-19th centuries AD.

NX444403. Signposted through arch mid-way along W side of the main street.

Historic Scotland; parish church in use.

Although the history of Christianity in Scotland probably began at Whithorn, the visitor to this unassuming town may not at first sense an atmosphere of spiritual antiquity, nor will he find the meaning of the ecclesiastical remains themselves immediately self-evident. There are four main visible objectives: the sites of the excavations in the glebe with their helpful display panels; the Museum at the corner of Bruce Street houses the important carved stones; within the churchyard there are the remains of the medieval cathedral-priory, the most prominent portion being the nave which was altered for post-Reformation use; and beyond that, the present parish church built in 1822 on the site of the east range of the medieval cloister.

These are disparate elements in a long and complicated story, and there are still considerable gaps in our knowledge, especially of its earliest phases. Despite the attentions of generations of archaeologists, Whithorn retains the quiet lure of a place whose rich seams of archaeological potential have not yet been worked out.

It was here that St Ninian, or Nynia, made his headquarters as bishop and missionary some time in the early 5th century, the first to be associated with the stone church or cathedral which, according to Bede, was known as the White House (*Ad Candida Casa*) and was dedicated to St Martin of Tours (d. 397). However, Christianity at Whithorn, and perhaps other pockets in south western Scotland was older than Ninian; how much older is not known, but his appointment was probably in response to an organised local community.

The actual location of the white-plastered (?and lime-mortared) *Candida Casa*, the first recorded church-building in Scotland, has long been a matter of debate. Unsubstantiated claims have been made in favour of Isle of Whithorn (no. 69); the current

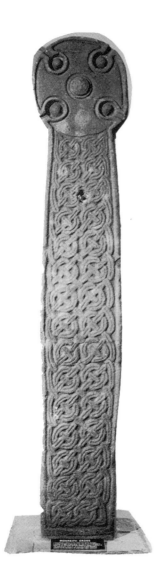

favourite, although it may equally belong to the 7th century, is the small building, now defined by modern dwarf-walls, at the eastern end of the crypt of the medieval cathedral-priory. When first uncovered, the roughly built walls were coated externally with a cream-coloured plaster. Excavations carried out in this vicinity are reported to have reached the earliest Christian levels; the only tangible evidence of the Ninianic period on public display, the inscribed pillar stone known as the *Latinus* stone, was also found in this general area in 1891. Ascribed to the mid 5th century by reason of the form and formula of the wording, it is the earliest Christian memorial in Scotland.

Information about the size and character of the monastery, which succeeded or formed part of the Ninianic church, has been enhanced by a series of large-scale excavations which have been carried out in the glebe to the south of the cathedral-priory. These have uncovered extensive remains of timber and stone buildings of the Anglian and Norse periods, as well as a large number of graves from medieval and earlier times. The archaeological discoveries, including rich craft-working material of the Norse period, are displayed in the nearby Visitor Centre in the High Street.

We can also be reasonably certain that the pillar stone known as the *Petrus* stone belongs to a Celtic monastic phase in the 7th century. It stood at the roadside about 400 m south of Whithorn, presumably within the monastic precinct. It bears an incised curvilinear cross with *chi-rho* symbol set within a double circle; the Latin inscription, cut in a rare form of Merovingian lettering, reads 'The place of Peter the apostle'.

Shortly before AD 731, the monastery was reconstituted as the centre of an Anglian bishopric, following the establishment of Northumbrian control in Galloway and, according to Bede, 'through increase of the ranks of the faithful'. There was a known succession of bishops throughout the 8th century, but thereafter the records fall silent until 1128. Our main body of historical evidence for the intervening centuries is in fact the group of carved stones in the museum. There are at least five, three cross-fragments and two slabs, which appear to belong exclusively to Northumbrian sculptural traditions of the 8th and 9th centuries. The rest are of a distinctive Whithorn 'school' of monuments, and belong to a period of Viking or Anglo-Norse control and settlement in the Machars from the early 10th century onwards. Of the Whithorn school, about twenty crosses would have served as headstones for individual graves, the majority having come from Whithorn. Only one survives complete, and only one bears a decipherable inscription (in runes): 'The monument [or cross] of Donferth'. The taller crosses are mainly from the surrounding district, marking religious centres and showing a respect on the part of Norse incomers for Christian places of burial. The most complete of these cemetery crosses is the 10th-century Monreith Cross which

**Whithorn
Museum:
Monreith Cross**
(Left)

Whithorn Priory: south wall of nave

stands 2.3 m high. Stylistically, the disc-headed form of the crosses is partly derived from the engraved circled cross long known in Galloway, while the patterns of interlace, the principal surface ornament, are Norse modifications of Northumbrian art. The cross-head typical of the Whithorn school has an embossed centrepiece and expanded curved arms with circular sunk 'armpits', sometimes also bossed in false relief.

The bishopric was revived in 1128, possibly at the instance of Fergus, Lord of Galloway, but the status of the community which served the restored see for the first fifty years is not clear. We do know, however, that a church of Romanesque style was erected in about the middle of the 12th century; its most unmistakeable feature is the ornamented south doorway at the west end of the nave where it was repositioned possibly in later medieval times. This Romanesque church was of cruciform plan with a short aisleless nave and an eastern arm of unknown extent, presumed long and aisled. There are contemporary fragments in the museum.

Whithorn's institutional history becomes clearer upon the introduction in about 1175-7 of Premonstratensian canons. By about 1235 the convent consisted of a prior and twenty canons, but numbers subsequently fluctuated, rising to about 25 in the early 16th century and down to about 16 in 1560. The architecture of the cathedral-priory is represented by 13th-century and later work in the nave and crypt at the east end. This church was rebuilt over and around its predecessor, incorporating some older details. The other south-facing doorway and most of the windows and tomb-recesses in the nave belong to this period; the relatively blank north side-wall flanked the cloister-garth. The present parish church occupies the northern end of the east range of the conventual buildings.

A special feature of the layout is the two-level arrangement at the east end. The eastern outline of the elaborate aisled choir is marked by modern walls, but the vaulted chambers of the crypt are intact and accessible. This two-storeyed treatment was dictated by the fall in ground level and by the need to provide space for St Ninian's shrine. The shrine attracted a considerable and lucrative pilgrimage traffic throughout the Middle Ages, probably second to none in Scotland. The last of the royal pilgrims was Queen Mary in 1563; by 1581 pilgrimages were formally prohibited.

At the Reformation the bishop and most of the canons, but not the prior, espoused the cause of the reformers. Until the final re-establishment of Presbyterianism in 1690 there was thus a succession of bishops, except in 1588-1605 and 1638-61. The revenues of the priory became reunited with the bishopric in 1605, and shortly afterwards the nave of the former cathedral-priory was repaired and rebuilt to suit the reformed liturgy. It served as a cathedral as long as Episcopacy prevailed, and from 1690 until 1822 its status was a parish church. The most substantial work undertaken in this period, probably early in the 18th century, was the remodelling and foreshortening of the west end following the collapse of the western tower. The frontal tower on the present parish church is an addition to the internally refurnished block of 1822.

PREHISTORIC RITUAL
AND FUNERARY MONUMENTS

**Torhousekie
stone circle**

The advent of Christianity was outwardly marked by changes in the commemoration and forms of human burial as well as in the liturgy and setting of religious worship. Cross-incised memorial stones are the most obvious point of departure, but it is not easy to gauge the extent to which symbols and sites sacred to more ancient societies were adapted for Christian purposes. The cross-incised standing stones at Laggangarn (no. 80), for example, are likely to be of prehistoric origin, but the antecedents of other groups of crosses and religious sites, including the holy caves and wells of western Galloway, remain incalculable. Some of the greatest changes were in burial practices: the inhumations were laid in consecrated cemeteries with no gravegoods to accompany them; they were extended in stone-lined cists, usually oriented east and west with the head at the west end, rather than crouched or cremated in short cists.

Whereas iron-age society is known mainly from its forts and settlements, it is by their burial practices and ceremonial that we know most about the earliest farming and metal-working communities in the south-west, namely those of neolithic and bronze-age times. Chambered tombs constitute the earliest and principal type of funerary monument of the neolithic period. The region has a few important outliers of the Clyde group of tombs, which, as their name suggests, are more typical of west central Scotland. Such tombs have distinctive slab-sided oblong chambers and archaeological examination of the long cairns at Cairnholy (no. 87) and Mid Gleniron (no. 89) are classic milestones in our understanding of the structure and function of this class of monument.

In the moorland areas, mainly around the valleys of the River Cree and the Water of Luce, there are about a dozen tombs which have simple megalithic chambers, but are otherwise more akin to passage-graves, the approach-passages merging into the chambers without any structural break. These tombs have been covered mainly by round cairns, though there are some long cairns of this type. They are known as Bargrennan tombs since their hybrid structural qualities and the distinctiveness of some of their associated pottery, were first recognised in the excavation of 'The White Cairn', Bargrennan (no. 88), in 1949.

The region also possesses a handful of apparently unchambered long cairns whose characteristics are less well known. Excavation at Lochhill (NX 968651) near New Abbey revealed that within the long cairn, 26.2 m by 11 m, there were remains of a timber-built and floored mortuary structure with an associated timber frontage, all later covered in stone. The mortuary timbers had been burnt, and radiocarbon dating of a plank registered a date of around 3700 BC.

The chambered tombs that have been examined show evidence of use and development over a long period. The last inhumations at Cairnholy I, for example, were in individual short cists associated with Beaker pottery and cup-and-ring-marked stones, traits characteristic of bronze-age communities. Cairns, presumably cisted and of the bronze age, are relatively common in the western uplands of the region, particularly on Creeside and in the Glenkens, but they are noticeably fewer in the east. The region is rich in metalwork finds dating from the middle bronze age, especially from about 1200 BC, and important hoards of weapons and implements have been discovered in Glentrool and at Drumcoltran. Alongside these strong metal-working and metal-using traditions, one of the most distinctive permanent legacies of late neolithic and bronze-age culture in this region is rock sculpture.

Argyll and Galloway are the two principal areas in which to find groups of cup and cup-and-ring markings in Scotland, and a recent catalogue lists 112 sites in Galloway where this rock art is known (nos 83 and 84; see also other notable sites at NX 452453, 696470). Their geographical distribution is concentrated mainly in three coastal areas: the Machars; the eastern side of the Cree estuary below Creetown; and an area between the Dee estuary and Dundrennan. There are northern outliers, but the distribution appears to have definite eastward and westward limits. Just what this decoration signifies has been the subject of much speculation, and the catalogue of Galloway sites appends no less than 104 theories that have been put forward to explain their meaning and use. They may have had some connection with metal-prospecting and smelting activities, or they may have had religious connotations, perhaps related to sun worship or other forms of astronomical observation.

Almost equally enigmatic, and exciting a similar range of mathematical and astronomical interpretations, are the stone circles and standing stones of the late neolithic and bronze-age periods. They are not especially numerous here, and they do not include any of the grand henge monuments

**Drumtroddan
standing stones**

characteristic of eastern and northern Scotland, but they do make up in quality what they lack in numbers. The setting of the eleven stones which form the circle of the 'Twelve Apostles' (no. 86) belies its true size which places it among the largest ceremonial circles in Britain. Some of the surviving circles of Galloway are of a locally distinctive, centre-stone type. The circles on Glenquicken Moor (NX 509582) and Claughreid (NX 517560) have massive central boulders circled by lesser stones, the former having 28 stones in a ring of 15.5 m diameter. The most complete of the Galloway circles, that at Torhousekie (no. 81), seems to be in the same tradition. However, its central setting comprises a small stone with two large flankers and a possible ring cairn behind, a layout reminiscent of the recumbent stone circles of north-east Scotland.

Visitors to Torhousekie will observe its relationship to outlying standing stones in its vicinity. Similar relationships can be seen elsewhere, as, for example, at the circle of Holm of Daltallochan (NX 553942). There are also numerous standing stones, apparently unrelated to circles or cairns, of which Drumtroddan (no. 82) and Laggangarn (no. 80) are the most conspicuous.

Among those standing stones credited with special associations, mention should be made of the so-called 'Taxing Stone' (NX 062709), which is believed to mark the burial-place of Alpin, King of Dalriada, killed in Glenapp. There is also the massive Clochmabanestane (NY 312659), the larger of two surviving granite boulders near the confluence of the Kirtle Water and the River Esk at the northern end of the Solway crossing, which may have formed part of a circle or enclosure. It is also arguable that this stone (tautologously called 'cloch' and 'stane') was the *Locus Maponi*, the tribal meeting-place or cult centre of the Celtic deity, Mabon (Roman Maponus or Apollo), mentioned in the 7th-century version of the Ravenna Cosmography, although Lochmaben itself has a rival claim. One thing is certain, and that is that the stone has been here for a very long time; charcoal from the underlying socket yielded a date of around 3200 BC.

80 Laggangarn, Standing Stones

2nd millennium BC and 7th-9th centuries AD.

NX 222716. Situated near the head of the Tarff Water and on the Southern Upland Way. From New Luce, N of Glenluce, take a minor road NE along the Water of Luce for 4 km to Balmurrie (NX 205665), whence there is a return trip of more than 11 km on foot. It is easy to lose the route over this stretch of afforested moorland, and visitors are strongly advised to consult the official guide to the Way.

Historic Scotland.

Lonely sentinals over a remote and afforested moorland, this closely-spaced pair of rough slabs now serves as a prominent landmark for travellers on the Southern Upland Way. Standing erect to heights of 1.88 m and 1.58 m, they each bear on the western face an incised Latin cross with tapered arms and, within the angles, four small crosses formed of intersecting lines. The larger crosses are of a style ascribable to the 7th-9th century AD, but the stones on which these Christian memorials have been carved are almost certainly of prehistoric origin.

Tradition asserts that there were once thirteen stones in the group, but just how many there may have been and whether they ever formed a circle has not been convincingly demonstrated.

81 Torhousekie, Stone Circle

2nd millennium BC.

NX 382564. On S side of B733, 5 km W of Wigtown; signposted.

Historic Scotland.

Set on a slightly raised platform in the gently undulating landscape of the Bladnoch valley, the stone circle at Torhousekie is one of the best preserved sites of its kind in Britain. It is unlike any of the other circles in the region, being more akin to some of the recumbent stone circles of north-east Scotland and south-west Ireland. It consists of nineteen granite boulders of somewhat dumpy proportions, graded in height towards the larger stones in the south-eastern sector, where the 21.6 m

diameter ring is noticeably 'flattened'. Near its centre there is a row of three stones aligned on a south-west/north-east axis, thus facing south-east; the smallish central stone is flanked by two massive boulders, and this central arrangement is backed by the remains of what has been interpreted as a D-shaped ring cairn. In 1684 Symson noted that these three stones were called 'King Galdus's tomb'.

A standing stone situated about 24 m to the south faces towards the circle, and to the east on the opposite side of the road at NX 384565 there is an alignment of three stones, evidently not part of another circle as was once thought.

82 Drumtroddan, Standing Stones

2nd millennium BC.

NX 364443. From the A 714 SW of Wigton, take farm track to Drumtroddan; in a field 0.7 km to the SE.

Historic Scotland.

Two out of an alignment of three tall standing stones stand clearly visible against the skyline, 3 m high, while the central member of the trio lies prostrate.

83 Drumtroddan, Cup-and-ring Markings

2nd millennium BC.

NX 362447. Railed enclosures in open field reached from farm track off A 714, SW of Wigtown.

Historic Scotland.

Several groups of markings have been found on the exposed faces of the greywacke outcrops on this open pastureland. There are cups, cups with rings, and some with connecting channels. The carvings show much variation in design, incorporating complete and gapped rings, and some with radial grooves. The maximum number of rings is six, and the greatest diameter within the fenced groups is 0.38 m. Another outcrop, 260 m south-south-west of the farm at NX 361446, includes a much weathered cup-and-five rings, 0.71 m in diameter.

Cup-and-ring
markings,
Drumtroddan

84 High Banks, Cup-and-ring Markings

2nd millennium BC.

NX 709489. SE of Kirkcudbright, in open pasture 400 m SE of High Banks Farm; the farm track can be reached from minor roads leading from the A 711 and B 727.

One of the best displays of prehistoric rock art in Galloway, this rock sheet, about 30 m long, bears several groups of cups and cups-and-rings. Some of the ringed cups are set within a field af massed simple cups, and their outer rings are widely spaced. The greatest ring diameter is 0.45 m.

Casts of this remarkable pattern are exhibited in the Stewartry Museum, Kircudbright, which also houses cup-and-rig marked slabs from Blackmyre (NX 497570) and Laggan (NX 5453).

85 'The Wren's Egg', Blairbuie, Standing Stones

Late 3rd-2nd millennia BC.

NX 361419. In field W of farm steading, track reached from minor road linking A 747 and A 714, SE of Port William.

This term of gentle irony is applied to a large granite boulder, a glacial erratic, which sits on the edge of a low ridge in a field north-east of Blairbuie Farmhouse. About 15 m east and downhill from the boulder is a pair of smaller standing stones, 1.5 m apart, whose relative positions gave rise to the belief that they were the surviving inner and outer elements of a double concentric stone circle centred on the 'Egg'. Survey and excavation have shown that a circle of any kind is unlikely to have existed here. The bases of the standing stones yielded meagre evidence of late 3rd and 2nd millennium activity.

86 'Twelve Apostles', Holywood, Stone Circle

3rd or 2nd millennium BC.

NX 947794. In field N of minor road which runs NW from New Bridge; leave A 76 at New Bridge or at junction with B 727.

Eleven out of a probable original twelve boulder stones, five of which are earthfast, make up this large 'flattened' circle. It is some 88 m in maximum diameter, but, spread over two low-lying enclosed fields close to the road, its position disguises the noteworthy fact that this is the largest stone circle on the Scottish mainland and the fifth largest in Britain. What has been the largest stone, 3.2 m long, lies wholly exposes in the south-western sector; the highest of the upright stones, about 1.9 m high, is set on a north-easterly alignment from it.

Close to the circle and visible only from the air as a long rectangle is another ceremonial monument, known as a curcus.

In 1837 it was reported that at Holm, about a mile to the east of the 'Apostles', there had been 'another Druidical temple' consisting of 'nine large stones', which had unfortunately been 'broken and applied to the purposes of building'.

'Twelve Apostles', Holywood: aerial view of stone circle with cursus in background

87 Cairnholy, Chambered Cairns

3rd and 2nd millennia BC.

NX 517538, 518540. Signposted from the A 75, SW of Gatehouse of Fleet, at Kirkdale Glen. From the car park at the lower site there is a short walk up the farm track to Cairnholy.

Historic Scotland.

On their hillside setting above Wigtown Bay, these two chambered tombs possess a range of dramatic visual qualities that are apparent under all lighting conditions. The lower or southern cairn (Cairnholy I) is quite majestic with its pillared eastern facade; set on a knoll some 150 m to the north, Cairnholy II is not so grand but its portals and inner capstone give it a more mysterious aspect. These tombs are the best of the Clyde group of long cairns in the region, and their excavation in 1949 produced a rich assemblage of finds (NMS).

Cairnholy I has been robbed of most of its overlying cairn material. In its final prehistoric form it was a long straight-sided mound, about 43 m by 10 m, aligned along the contour and extending beyond the present road. The inner burial-chamber with its massive side-slabs probably represents the nucleus of the tomb, and was covered with a small cairn. To this was later added an ante-chamber, and then a concave 'horned' facade comprising eight tall pillars. The forecourt seems to have been designed as a setting for ritual ceremonies. At least six fires had been lit in this area before it was blocked for good, and indications of pottery-associated offerings were uncovered. A fragment of jadeite axe-blade found in the outer compartment may also have been related to these ceremonies.

There is a large slab in the inner chamber which bears a weathered cup-mark with four or five concentric rings; it possibly roofed the last (cist) burial within this compartment. A small cup-and-ring-marked slab found in the inner chamber is now in NMS.

The cairn which originally covered Cairnholy II has been much denuded, leaving only its irregular oblong outline around the summit of the hillock. Most of the stones evidently went into the construction of dykes and buildings in the late 18th century, but robbing stopped at the large slabs of the tomb itself. It consists of slab-sided inner and outer (perhaps secondary) chambers, the inner still retaining its large capstone. The entrance is flanked by tall and leaning portal stones, one 2.9 m high, the other possibly broken; like Cairnholy I, it had a large closing stone, now recumbent. Excavated finds from the outer compartment included a leaf-shaped arrowhead, a flint knife and Beaker pottery, thus showing a similar range of users to that of the neighbouring tomb.

Cairnholy I : forecourt

chambered cairn
(Top)

**Cairnholy II
chambered cairn**

88* Bargrennan, 'The White Cairn', Chambered Cairn

3rd millennium BC.

NX 352783. From Bargrennan on the A 714, 13 km NW of Newton Stewart, take minor road NE to Glentrool Village; cairn in forestry plantation to W of village, access restricted.

Forestry Commission.

Now surrounded by forestry plantations, this much-reduced circular cairn has given its name to a group of about a dozen passage-graves of localised distribution in this area. The cairn has a diameter of 13.7 m, and in the centre stands to a maximum height of 1.4 m. Excavation in 1949 showed that the centre of the cairn contained a megalithic chamber and south-facing passage which were structurally undifferentiated. In a ritual fire-pit near the entrance cremated bones were mixed with abundant fragments of oak charcoal, whilst finds (from the passage) comprised up to 60 small sherds of an unusual variety of late neolithic pottery.

89 Mid Gleniron, Chambered Cairns

Late 4th-2nd millennia BC.

NX 186610, 187609. on either side of track to Mid Gleniron Farm, E of Glenluce-New Luce road, some 2 km N of Glenluce Abbey (no. 72).

Excavation of these two long chambered tombs in 1963-6 revealed a multi-period structural sequence of some complexity and provided a better understanding of the development of Clyde cairns in general. They are in somewhat mutilated condition and their special significance is thus historical rather than visual.

Mid Gleniron I (NX 186610) originated in a small rectangular burial chamber (the northernmost), which was contained within a small cairn of probable early neolithic date. A second chamber in a small cairn was then built independently in front of it. Finally, a third chamber was set laterally between the two, all three being joined into a long straight-sided mound with a crescentic north facade. Nine cremations in cinerary urns had been inserted into the south-eastern flank, showing that the cairn had subsequently been used as a burial place in bronze-age times.

The much-ruined Mid Gleniron II, 120 m to the south-east, is likewise of multi-period construction. It originated in an oval cairn with an eastward-facing small chamber. A larger, south-facing chamber was then added, the enlarged composite structure being enclosed within a straight-sided cairn with southern facade. The later chamber no longer survives.

To the south of each of the long cairns is a circular burial cairn, that to the south of Mid Gleniron II being a large circular mound about 17 m in diameter and 2.75 m high. Excavation brought to light a small closed box-like chamber at the centre, the whole structure possibly being comtemporary with the nearby chambered tombs. The much-disturbed cairn to the south of Mid Gleniron I yielded a cremated human bone, perhaps originally contained within a cinerary urn. The finds from the excavations are in Dumfries Museum.

MUSEUMS AND VISITOR CENTRES

The two largest and most important site museums are those at Whithorn (no. 79) and Wanlockhead (no. 9). The collections in Burns' House, Dumfries (no. 11), the 'Arched House', Ecclefechan (no. 17), and Ellisland Farm (no. 21) are of social as well as literary interest. Shambellie (no. 22) is the setting for a museum of historic costumes, whilst Craigcleuch (NY 343869), near Langholm, serves as the Scottish Explorers' Museum. The control tower of the former military airfield at Heathhall, Dumfries (NY 0079), one of ten local sites operational in the 1939-45 war, is the centrepiece of the Dumfries and Galloway Aviation Museum. The Galloway Deer Museum on the shore of Clatteringshaws Loch at NX 552763 contains an unexpected and informative display on the archaeology of the area; nearby is a reconstructed iron-age hut.

There are small local collections of artefacts at Annan, Moffat, and elsewhere. The principal town museums are:

Dumfries Museum, Church Street. The most extensive and important collection of archaeological material of all periods relating to the whole region. Part of the museum incorporates an observatory tower, formerly a windmill, in which a camera obscura was installed in 1836.

Kirkcudbright. The Stewartry Museum, St Mary Street. Notable multi-period collection displayed inside and outside purpose-built structure of 1892.

Newton Stewart. The Museum (formerly St John's Church), York Road. A recently established (1978) but growing collection, mainly illustrating social life of recent centuries.

**Drumlanrig
Castle**

BIBLIOGRAPHY

Andrew, K *The Southern Upland Way, Western Section*, HMSO, Edinburgh, 1984.

Breeze, DJ *Roman Scotland: a guide to the visible remains*, Newcastle upon Tyne, 1979.

Brooke, D *Wild Men and Holy Places*, Edinburgh, 1994.

Cassidy, B (ed.) *The Ruthwell Cross*, Princeton, 1992.

Cowan, IB, and Easson, DE *Medieval Religious Houses, Scotland*, London, 1976.

Cruden, S *The Scottish Castle*, Edinburgh, 1981.

Dick, CH *Highways and Byways in Galloway and Carrick*, London, 1916.

Donnachie, I *The Industrial Archaeology of Galloway*, Newton Abbot, 1971.

Donnachie, I, and Macleod, I *Old Galloway*, Newton Abbot, 1974.

Dunbar, JG *The Historic Architecture of Scotland*, London, 1966; revised edition, 1978.

Fawcett, R *Scottish Medieval Churches*, Edinburgh, 1985.

Harper, MM *Rambles in Galloway*, Edinburgh, 1876.

Hay, G *The Architecture of Scottish Post-Reformation Churches 1560-1843*, Oxford, 1957.

Henshall, AS *The Chambered Tombs of Scotland*, vol. 2, Edinburgh, 1972.

Hume, JR *The Industrial Archaeology of Scotland: 1 The Lowlands and Borders*, London, 1976.

McDowall, W *History of the Burgh of Dumfries*, Edinburgh, 1867; third edition, 1906.

MacGibbon, D, and Ross, T *The Castellated and Domestic Architecture of Scotland*, Edinburgh, 5 vols, 1887-92.

MacGibbon, D, and Ross, T *The Ecclesiastical Architecture of Scotland*, Edinburgh, 3 vols, 1896-7.

McKerlie, PH *History of the Lands and their Owners in Galloway*, Edinburgh, 5 vols, 1870-8; Paisley, 2 vols, 1906.

Mackenzie, WM *The Medieval Castle in Scotland*, London, 1927.

MacKie, EW *Scotland: an Archaeological Guide*, London, 1975.

Macleod, I *Discovering Galloway*, Edinburgh, 1985.

MacTaggart, J *The Scottish Gallovidian Encyclopaedia*, London, 1824.

Maxwell, H *A History of Dumfries and Galloway*, Edinburgh, 1896.

Morris, RWB *Prehistoric Rock Art of Galloway and the Isle of Man*, Poole, 1979.

Piggott, S *Scotland Before History*, Edinburgh, 1982.

Pryde, GS, and Duncan, AAM *The Burghs of Scotland, A critical list*, Glasgow, 1965.

Ritchie, G & A *Scotland: Archaeology and Early History*, Edinburgh, 1991.

Robertson, AS *Birrens (Blatobulgium)*, Edinburgh, 1975.

Rowan, A *The Creation of Shambellie*, HMSO, Edinburgh, 1982.

Royal Commission on the Ancient and Historical Monuments of Scotland,
An Inventory of the Monuments ... in the County of Wigtown, HMSO, Edinburgh, 1912.

An Inventory of the Monuments ... in the County of the Stewartry of Kirkcudbright, HMSO, Edinburgh, 1914.

An Inventory of the Monuments ... in the County of Dumfries, HMSO, Edinburgh, 1920.

Archaeological Sites and Monuments Series, *nos 12* (Upper Eskdale, 1980), *13* (Ewesdale and Lower Eskdale, 1981), *and 24* (West Rhins, 1985).

Scott, JG *South-West Scotland*, London, 1966.

Symson, A *A large description of Galloway*, (1684; revised 1692) contained in eg Mitchell, A (ed.), Macfarlane's Geographical Collections, vol 2, Edinburgh, 1907.

Taylor, W *The Military Roads in Scotland*, Newton Abbot, 1976.

Thomas, C *The Early Christian Archaeology of North Britain*, Glasgow and London, 1971.

Torrie, EPD, and Coleman, R *Historic Stranraer*, Aberdeen, 1995.

Tranter, N *The Fortified House in Scotland*, *vol. 3*, Edinburgh, 1965.

Urquhart, J *Dumfries and Galloway: Our Story in Pictures*, Dumfries, 1972.

Wood, JM *Smuggling in the Solway*, Dumfries, 1908.

There are also guide booklets or leaflets to individual monuments in the care of Historic Scotland:

Caerlaverock Castle;
Cardoness Castle;
Drumcoltran Castle;
Dundrennan Abbey;
MacLellan's Castle,
Kirkcudbright;
Lincluden Collegiate Church;
New Abbey Corn Mill;
Ruthwell Cross;
Sweetheart Abbey;
Threave Castle;
Whithorn (including Chapel Finian,
Kirkmadrine,
Laggangarn,
St Ninian's Cave and St Ninian's Chapel).

Mull of Galloway

INDEX OF PLACES

Printed in Scotland for The Stationery Office by (3808)
Dd 293090 C50 10/96